John Lewis-Stempel ma........................n, after reading an article in the Young Ornithologists' Club's magazine. He has written on gardening and wildlife for numerous publication including .... *Design* and *Grow Your Own*, has been a full-time gardener, and worked for a conservation charity. In 2012 he received a Society of Authors' Foundation Award for his writings on nature. As well as keeping a wildlife garden, he runs an organic farm. His other books include *The Wild Life: A Year of Living on Wild Food* and *Foraging: The Essential Guide to Free Wild Food*.

Other titles from *Right Way* and *How To Books*

THE WILDLIFE GARDEN

John Lewis-Stempel

Constable & Robinson Ltd
55–56 Russell Square
London WC1B 4HP
www.constablerobinson.com

First published in the UK by How To Books,
an imprint of Constable & Robinson Ltd, 2014

A copy of the British Library Cataloguing in Publication
Data is available from the British Library

ISBN 978-0-71602-349-4 (paperback)
ISBN 978-0-71602-355-5 (ebook)

Printed and bound in the UK

1 3 5 7 9 10 8 6 4 2

'Nobody made a greater mistake than he who did nothing because he could do only a little.'

Edmund Burke

CONTENTS

ACKNOWLEDGEMENTS

The author and publisher wish to thank The Mammal Society for permission to reproduce the image of the small mammal footprint tube on page 151, and the Bat Conservation Trust for permission to reproduce the image of the construction plan of the bat box on page 133.

PREFACE

Gardens are an increasingly important refuge for the nation's wildlife. Often more 'friendly' than farmland, they are now the main habitat for endangered species such as the song thrush and stag beetle. A typical garden can be home to twenty or more species of bird, five of mammal, several of amphibians and hundreds of invertebrates. A wildlife-friendly garden can easily, and unbelievably, be home to more than 5,000 species of fauna and flora. Per square metre, a wildlife-friendly garden is more biodiverse than the Amazon rainforest! This is because good gardens have an array of physical structures (from trees to fences), diverse micro-habitats, are constantly being remade by digging and contain an artificially high diversity of plants.

Making a garden wildlife friendly is doing your bit for Britain's animals and plants. Domestic gardeners have a crucial role to play in the future of our wildlife; back gardens make up four per cent of Britain's land surface, the same as Sites of Special Scientific Interest. It also helps make your garden fit for humans too. A wildlife garden is uplifting, a place of beauty, of inspiration and of pleasure, where all the senses are appealed to. A garden that is green and 'natural' is proven to be better for your mental and physical health. A garden where a robin will perch on your hand to feed is a garden where children can properly appreciate the natural world.

Currently in vogue, wildlife gardening is actually a throwback to a pre-chemical, less formalistic gardening style. A traditional cottage garden was heaven on earth for butterflies and bees, and it's not difficult to make. It really only requires you to give nature a helping hand. Neither is wildlife gardening an all or nothing creed. Wildlife gardening is not a religion, but a pragmatic solution for humans and nature to share the same space. With a little know-how and energy, any garden, no matter how small, can be a haven for wildlife. Many gardens, indeed, will only need tweaking to maximise their wildlife potential.

Your garden. Where the wild things can be.

CHAPTER 1
PLANNING THE WILDLIFE GARDEN

'Wildlife' and 'garden' are often assumed to be opposites. After all, this way of thinking goes, wildlife likes long grass and informality, while gardeners like shaved lawns and order. Wildlife likes 'organic', gardeners like chemicals. Wildlife likes sprawling hawthorn hedges, gardeners like trimmed conifers.

And too many people assume that a wildlife garden is an area behind the house left to go native. This would not be a garden; this would be a scrubland wilderness. Funnily enough, it would not be as species-rich as even a moderately wildlife-friendly garden. A wildlife garden needs maintenance by people.

Other misconceptions abound: a wildlife garden does not have to be the size of Surrey to be effective. To a bee, a window box is a nectar hypermarket. *Whatever* the size of your garden, whether it's a kitchen window in a flat or a sprawling, broad acre in the country, you can easily do something for wildlife. Everybody can help.

Planning a wildlife-friendly garden is not essentially different from planning any other form of garden. It is about what you want the garden to look like, what it needs to do – a play area for the kids, a massive vegetable patch for self-sufficiency, a quiet retreat for creativity – and working with the lie of the land. You also have to ask yourself a key question: how committed to wildlife are you? Do you want to do something for wildlife or everything for wildlife? How you answer the question is entirely up to you, but there are some simple rules every wildlife gardener should follow ...

THE TEN WILDLIFE GARDEN COMMANDMENTS

1. **Plant plants, plants**

   Plants, plants, plants are the three most important words in wildlife gardening. Green as much of your garden as you are able to (not forgetting vertical spaces such as house walls and fences) with as great a diversity of plants as possible. Ideally you should choose native species, not least because this increases the native floral 'reservoir', but this is not a rule etched in stone. A hungry bird is as happy with firethorn berries as hawthorn berries. (That said, avoid modern, super-bred cultivars because few contain pollen or nectar.) Choose a range of plants to feed as many animals as possible over the course of the year.

2. **Stop using chemicals**

   Pesticides can annihilate crucial layers of the food chain. There are other effective ways to keep pests and weeds under control. Learn to love bugs. Most are your friends.

3. **Provide food and shelter for birds and beasties**

   To encourage birds into the garden, put up seed and peanut feeders and erect artificial shelters. Then grow natural food and cover. Other animals can also be fed, from hedgehogs to butterflies and bees. But always keep up feeding regimes. Make a wildlife hotel for creepy crawlies. Microfauna – microscopic animals in the soil – are interesting in their own right, often beneficial, and are a key stage in the garden food chain.

4. **Give Tiddles a bell**

   The UK's cats kill 55 million birds a year. There is no evidence that cat predation is actually causing the decline in bird numbers, but with some garden species (notably the song thrush and tree sparrow) already under pressure it is prudent to give a cat a bell so potential feathered prey can hear it coming – but the cat's collar should be of a proper fit, and have a safety feature such as an elastic insert ('stretch collar') so the cat can free itself if it becomes entangled.

5. **Make a pond**
   Any pond, whether it's a bird bath or something you can swim in. Adding a water feature to the garden massively increases diversity in the species that live and visit there. (But don't put fish in the pond – they will eat all the many other animals.)

6. **Do not prune bushes or cut hedges between March and August**
   This is the main nesting season for birds, and few will tolerate disturbance when sitting on eggs or raising young.

7. **Compost**
   Composting garden and raw vegetable/fruit waste saves the environment, nourishes the soil and provides a micro-habitat.

8. **Let the grass grow**
   Most lawns are green deserts. Even a patch of lawn that is allowed to grow and sprout wildflowers will be a wonderland for insects. Amphibians, birds and small mammals will follow.

9. **Pile up some logs**
   It's not the most glamorous way of saving wildlife, but for a quick wildlife garden 'fix' plonking logs on top of each other is almost unrivalled. Pick a sheltered, shady space, and very soon the log pile will be a wooden wonder of fungi, mosses, insects and other invertebrates, together with small mammals and amphibians. What the log pile is doing is mimicking the woodland habitat. A lot of the best of wildlife gardening is exactly that: mimicking nature.

10. **Don't tidy too much**
    A phrase you are unlikely to hear in any other context. Tidiness is the enemy of wildlife gardening. Allow leaves on the lawn. Let seed heads stay on stalks. Don't repair every gap of mortar in the garden wall. Let the nettles grow untroubled in a small corner. Yes, really – nettles are host to butterflies and moth larvae. You can cut them and let them stew in water for a fine organic fertiliser, or indeed as a green vegetable, beer or tea for you. You are entitled to enjoy the floral benefits of the garden too.

A little forethought means you can make a better garden for you and wildlife. Most people will inherit a garden, rather than start with a *tabula rasa*. Take account of the existing flora and fauna. A *leylandii* hedge is not fantastic for wildlife; however simply ripping it out in favour of a deciduous alternative will rob your existing birds of a roosting and nesting site. Drive a creature away and it may not come back. Only remove a conifer when you have a well-established substitute.

Generally, take your wildlife planning cues from the style of the surrounding land. Your garden, ideally, can connect with others to form enlarged habitats. If a neighbour has a woodland glade and you can create an adjoining one, the wildlife value will be more than the sum of the two parts. A hedge leading to another hedge makes an ideal 'green corridor' for a hedgehog to wander along and increase its hunting range.

Find out about the wildlife of the area. If you know what species the garden is likely to attract, you can ensure a warm welcome for them. Your local gardening centre or gardening club should be able to help.

Diversity is good. Try to make as many mini-habitats that mimic nature as the garden will bear. Try to plan in vertical 'storeys' because changes in height maximise wildlife appeal and human interest. Dividing the garden by walls, arches and flower borders creates the illusion of space as well as creating areas with different 'feels'; divisions also give privacy to animals. Most animals are prey and need cover. They do not like wide open spaces.

If you have children consider corners where they can sit, read or play in a natural environment. And so they can *look* at nature. Wildlife gardens are exciting places for children to learn about – and experience – the natural world at first hand rather than via a screen.

And, whatever you do, plan in a decent path if the garden is likely to have a good deal of traffic from one end to the other. Begin by getting the shape right, then consider how you can improve the path's 'wildlife value'. For instance, stepping stones with small chambers underneath for amphibians work well for man and mini-beast.

Deciding what you want from a garden, then finding the animal-friendly way of achieving it, is the very essence of successful wildlife gardening without tears.

STEP-BY-STEP: PLAN THE WILDLIFE GARDEN

Step 1. Understand your soil. Soils vary from area to area. Trying to grow plants that love dry chalky soil on wet clay is unlikely to be fruitful. A DIY soil testing kit, which can be bought for as little as £10, will give the pH of the soil, meaning its acidity or alkalinity.

Step 2. Draw a rough scale plan, indicating on it any existing features you wish to keep.

Step 3. On the same plan sketch in any necessary 'family-friendly' features you wish to add, such as a clothes line, trampoline or barbecue area.

Step 4. What garden features do you want? A large herbaceous border? A herb garden? A pergola?

Step 5. Are there any natural features that could be taken advantage of? A soggy patch where the water table comes close to the surface would be ideal for a bog garden.

Step 6. Now plan in the three infrastructural commandments: a water body, a compost heap and a log pile.

Step 7. Plan in a path.

Step 8. Decide what animals you want to live in or be attracted to the garden. Don't forget those that already live in the garden.

Step 9. Use this book to see which plants and micro-habitats will lure and provide for the chosen fauna.

Step 10. And then use this book to reconcile any conflicts and expand the wildlife potential of the garden.

Step 11. Be realistic too about how much time you have for gardening. Revise your plan accordingly.

Getting it right will be easier than you think. Not enough space on the lawn for a pond? Make a container pond for the patio. Want a large luscious herbaceous border but are pinched for space? Good. Simply plant native and insect-friendly plants in *tiers*.

The wildlife garden does not have to be 'designed' to the nth degree; you do not need to have the landscape flair of Capability Brown and the zoological know-how of David Attenborough. Or, indeed, to spend weeks with tape measures, theodolites and squared paper. There are some *easy* measures that can make an immediate aesthetic and wildlife difference to any garden, and many are included in this book, from greening a garden shed to making a wildlife hotel for insects. But a good wildlife garden grows over years.

Tip: Before you absolutely finalise your plan or proposed adaptions, picture them in the different seasons. Do they fulfil your needs all year round? And the needs of wildlife?

THE TOP TEN PLANTS FOR THE WILDLIFE GARDEN

Ice plant *Sedum spectabile*
Small, tough and can be grown almost anywhere, from the roof to the herbaceous border, via the rockery. The ice plant provides nectar late in the season and is a haven for hoverflies, bees and butterflies.

Buddleia *Buddleia davidii*
A shrub known as the butterfly bush for its astonishing ability to attract the Lepidoptera order.

Sunflower *Helianthus*
The heads provide a brilliant burst of sunshine in the summer and a buffet of seeds for birds in the autumn.

Thyme *Thymus*
Usefully, this familiar kitchen herb also provides good ground cover for invertebrates, and bees tuck into its nectar.

Lavender *Lavandula*
Produces a fragrance intoxicating to humans and flying insects alike. When the purple flowers go to seed they provide a banquet for birds. It comes in dwarf versions, making it suitable for patios, window boxes, containers and hanging baskets.

Ivy *Hedera*
A much overlooked plant, yet close to essential in the wildlife garden. Holly blue caterpillars eat the flowers, buds and berries, while butterflies and hoverflies take nectar from the flowers. Birds eat the berries. Birds nest and roost in its foliage. Invertebrates winter in its evergreen recesses. It will tolerate almost any soil, and can be grown up walls and fences. A plant for a no space garden and a big garden alike.

Firethorn *Pyracantha*
Slightly gaudy red-berried shrub, which is as loved by wildlife for its nectar, fruit and thick shelter as it is hated by burglars for its thorns. Excellent as hedging.

Primrose *Primula vulgaris*
A classic British plant, the blooming of which is a sure sign of spring, and a source of early nectar for bees and butterflies. A good

wildlife garden should supply nectar for as much of the insect flying season as possible.

Silver birch *Betula pendula*

Have room for a tree? The silver birch is a long-established native of these shores (the first tree to re-colonise the country after the last Ice Age). It doesn't grow too tall, and its silver-white colour together with drooping catkins provide a charming arboreal aesthetic. On top of this, it is the life support system for no less than 334 insect species, which in turn attract feathered predators galore. Its open canopy lets light through, and wildflowers will thrive at the base. An alternative for a very small garden is the ornamental crab apple (*malus*).

Purple coneflower *Echinacea purpurea*

Attractive upright perennial with large daisy-like flower heads which brings colour – and pints of nectar – to any garden. A flower lover's flower.

WHAT NOT TO DO: THE WILDLIFE-UNFRIENDLY GARDEN

The 'typical' suburban garden (opposite) could be worse; it could be completely covered in concrete or decking. But much of it is open desert, a sterile environment of use to very few species; the grass of the lawn is too short, the fences are bare of greenery, the pond is full of fish and has little nearby cover. The same garden can easily be made more wildlife friendly.

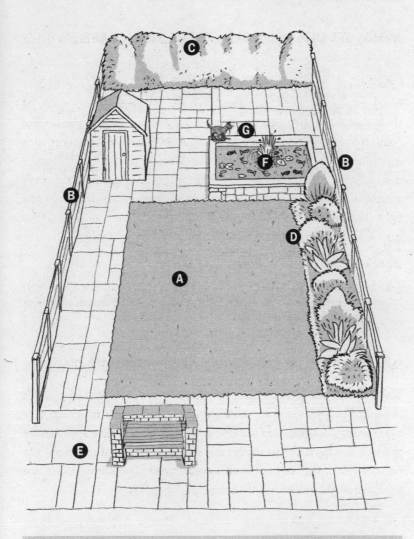

Key

A Manicured lawn

B Bare fences

C *Leylandii*

D Thin flower border full of non-native, modern cultivars

E Extensive slab patio

F Formal pond with few plants, inaccessible sides and hungry fish

G Cats without collars

WHAT TO DO: THE WILDLIFE-FRIENDLY GARDEN

Key

A Lawn allowed to grow over spring and summer into a wildflower meadow; a shaved section is left for the children's swing

B Wide flower borders with mostly native species of plant, providing nectar, berries, roosting and nesting sites

C Ornamental crab apple trees with bird nest boxes

D Log and rock pile

E Small pond, planted with native flowers (and no fish)

F Compost heap, providing nutrients for the garden, and its own micro-habitat

G Slab path, with chambers for amphibians underneath: creeping thyme and other plants grow in the spaces between the slabs

H Bog garden

I Garden shed with green roof of ice plant; the shed can also be used as a hide. Water from the roof is collected in a water butt

J Creeper-covered fences with strategically placed bird boxes

K Bay tree in container

L Herb garden in a raised bed on patio

M Wild 2m x 2m nettle patch

N Patio with bird table and feeders, so birds eating can be clearly seen from house

O Hedge of native species, including hawthorn and blackthorn

P Wildlife hotel to attract beneficial predators

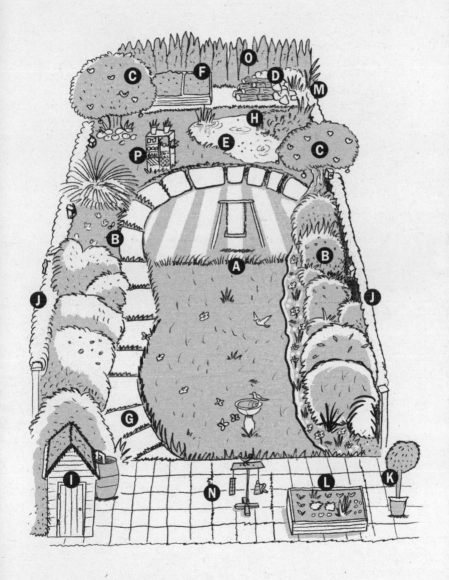

CHAPTER 2
LAWNS

A lawn, when you come to think of it, is nothing but a meadow in captivity. When the British moved off the land in the nineteenth century to work in factories and towns, they could not quite bear to leave behind their rural roots and so created a patch of familiar green behind the house. Alas, modern lawns have little wildlife value. Most are marinated in chemicals and comprised of only a couple of grass species. They are shorn to within a centimetre of their life by whirling cutting blades up to once a week in summer.

Do something wild. Whatever the size of your lawn, you can make it more wildlife friendly and in return enjoy the satisfied buzz of bees, the chirp of crickets, flutter of butterflies and the glorious evensong of the thrush family. All this, and have a practical lawn for family use. Of course, if you have space you could go the whole hedgehog and have a wildflower lawn.

Almost all of Britain's traditional wildflower hay meadows have been lost under intensive agriculture in the last fifty years. Humans have been deprived of one of nature's glories. For native pollinators and other fauna it has been a biodiversity holocaust. A wildflower lawn, no matter how small, can help halt the decline.

MAKING A LAWN WILDLIFE FRIENDLY

To turn a lawn into a wildlife habitat, less really is best.
- Ban any form of weedkiller and fertiliser.
- Reduce the frequency of mowing, remove all cut grass (to reduce the lawn's fertility, allowing wild grasses and flowers

to grow) and set the blades higher, and improvement will quickly follow.

- Better still, let the grass grow long. If your lawn is also a play space, a compromise is easy. Mow most of the lawn to ball-playing acceptability, but leave shaggy uncut borders at the sides. Wild fauna like corridors and continuous stretches to perambulate. At the very least leave the grass at the base of trees uncut. Very small children can be bribed into accepting long grass by mowing paths in a 'maze' design for them to follow.
- Cut the long grass in August when the seeds have set.

A WILDFLOWER LAWN

Wildflowers in a lawn are things of singular beauty and colour. One method of adding them to your lawn is by overseeding in autumn with a commercial wildflower mix. To do this, cut the lawn as low as possible, then rake rigorously to remove debris and to scratch small bare patches. Mix the seeds with a little sand and broadcast thinly, then rake in.

In truth, you may be disappointed with the results, because grass can be a rampant smotherer of tender flowers. A surer way of upping the wildflower quotient of the lawn is to plant out plugs of young plants directly. Again, plugs are available commercially, although many gardeners prefer to propagate the seeds themselves. A plug gives a wildflower a head start. Mow the lawn closely in spring, and dig a hole for the plug with a trowel. If you have some bare patches or mole hills, where the grass has been set back, so much the better for your wildflower plugs. Put some compost in the bottom of the hole and water well.

Where you live will govern to a great extent what wildflowers will thrive on your lawn. That said, there are few places where cowslips, red clover and ox-eye daisies will not establish themselves plentifully. Arrange the plants in groups of three to five to get a natural effect. Mow with the setting on high once a month to reduce the competition from the grass, with the exception of the summer when the grass should be 'let go'. To prevent the lawn looking as though you have lazily forgotten about it, you can mow a path across it.

Within three years your lawn should have been transformed into a delight to the eye and nose, as well as a haven for wildlife. It will have changed from a lawn with wildflowers to a wildflower lawn.

Tip: Try a simple experiment to see what benefits a change in lawn regime will have. Peg out one metre square of lawn and let the grass grow and flower. You will be amazed by the range of insects that will live in your pocket meadow, and the birds, and possibly amphibians and small mammals.

While you are in the long grass look out for a little patch of foam or 'cuckoo-spit' clinging to the tall stalks. If the foam is smeared out, you will find a pale greeny-yellow creature inside, which is the nymph of the common frog-hopper. The 'spit' is produced by the larva blowing bubbles from its anus to keep itself moist and hidden from predators. As the frog-hopper's name implies, its outsize back legs when adult do indeed enable it to hop. On a good day *Philaenus spumarius* is the world's greatest jumper, leaping as high as 70cm – the equivalent of a human jumping over the Great Pyramid of Giza. To do this, the little brown bug attains an initial acceleration of 4,000 metres per second. The gravitational force exerted on the body at this point is 400G – 80 times that exerted on an astronaut being launched into orbit.

STEP-BY-STEP: MAKING A WILDFLOWER MEADOW FROM SCRATCH

If you don't already have a lawn, or if you have time to put in the extra work, it is highly enjoyable to create your wildflower meadow from scratch. Most grassland wildflowers thrive on an open aspect, so choose somewhere sunny. Curiously, wildflowers thrive on nutrient-poor soil, their beauty and profusion in almost inverse proportion to the richness of the earth.

Step 1. Preparation

Begin by outlining the shape of the lawn with ropes. Unless you have a particularly threadbare existing lawn or chalky, stony soil, you will need to remove one to two inches of topsoil, ensuring you dig deep enough to remove the existing grass's roots. If this seems like potentially back-breaking labour, you might want to hire a mini-digger. A method that is lighter on the back and arms, albeit time-consuming, is to put the land down to mustard or oil-seed rape for a season to reduce fertility, removing the crop at flowering time. Whichever method you choose you then need to:

- Rotovate or dig the soil on the prepared area, then firm and rake to make a seedbed.
- Allow six weeks for the soil to settle and for any weed seeds to germinate.
- Hoe any weed seeds off before sowing. With very pernicious weeds you might, for one time only, use a weed-killer. But use one based on glyphosate, such as Tumbleweed or Roundup, which have relatively low toxicity and deactivate on contact with the soil.

Tip: On heavy soils, prepare and sow during March and April, as waterlogging over winter may cause autumn-sown seedlings to rot. On lighter soils, autumn-sown seeds should establish quickly.

Step 2. Sowing

Seed for a wildflower meadow can be purchased ready mixed, or you can concoct your own (see below) to suit your tastes and local conditions. Whatever you sow, the mix needs to be about 50 per cent grass and 50 per cent wildflower seed. (Ignore any recommendations of 20 per cent wildflower seeds to 80 per cent grass. Whatever the weather conditions or soil suitability, the wildflower seeds will suffer a significant casualty rate.)

Ensure the grass component is varied, and contains traditional grasses such as fescue (*Festuca glauca*), timothy (*Phleum pratense*) and cocksfoot (*Dactylis glomerata*).

Another good idea is to put yellow rattle (*Rhinanthus minor*) seed in the mix. Yellow rattle, a traditional plant of British wildflower meadows, is semi-parasitic on grass. Others useful in controlling grass are the *Pedicularis* and *Euphrasia* species. These parasitic plants sap the vigour of the grasses, and allow wildflowers to flourish.

Wildflower seeds are often tiny so a little silver sand in the mixture will help handling.

- Sow the mix at the rate of 15g/m². Sparse sowing plus the yellow rattle seeds will mean that the grasses won't crowd out the wildflowers.
- Large areas up to an acre can be sown by hand quite easily. To ensure an even broadcast sow half widthways and half lengthways.
- Rake in, and water thoroughly. Cover with netting if hungry birds and the neighbour's cat's loo habits are a problem.

Tip: While the lawn is growing, mow an access path across it; this saves tramping the grass down when you need to cross the lawn, as well as providing somewhere you can watch wildlife from.

Step 3. Maintaining

You can choose to have a spring or summer wildflower lawn. This is determined by what flowers you choose (see below), and when you cut the grass.

Spring-flowering meadows should be cut in June and for the remainder of the summer. They are left to grow from February until June.

Summer meadows are cut in August, after most flowers have ripened their seeds. Over the autumn and early winter they are mown at least four times. They are left to grow from March to August.

Whatever time you cut, your mower will struggle with the 30cm high grass and flowers, so you will need to use a strimmer. Or you could use a hand scythe, which is non-polluting and quick – once you have mastered the knack. The charity Butterfly Conservation recommends using a power scythe; these are rather pricey, however.

A wildflower meadow or lawn should never be cut below 5cm. Some butterflies, notably skippers, spend the winter as a chrysalis on the lowest stems of grasses. After the big July or August cut, leave the mowings in place for a few days to allow seeds to drop to the ground. The grass then needs to be taken away. Put it on the compost heap, or pile up as a habitat itself (snakes love the warmth of rotting grass). You could even have a go at making hay.

On subsequent trims, remove all grass. These trims are meant to emulate a sheep or cow, since in traditional hay meadows a farmer would put on livestock to have a 'bite' of the grass between summer and winter. If you don't have sheep, mowing is the most environmentally friendly way to manipulate the range of wildflowers.

Tip: Always leave a small border uncut so that the insects and small vertebrates you disturb when mowing can retreat to safety.

MAKING HAY

As mentioned above, an option for your long grass, besides putting it on the compost heap and letting it rot down, is to make hay. This can be very handy if you have herbivorous pets. Few things in life are more satisfying than making hay, and few things are more nutritious for your pet than the hay you will make.

The old adage is true: you 'make hay when the sun shines'. Pick a sunny three-day window in the weather. Cut the grass with a strimmer or scythe, preferably late morning when the dew has been burned off. Leave the mown grass where it lies for several hours, then turn it over with a wide-headed rake so the bottom grass comes up to the sun to be dried.

You will need to repeat the drying–turning action (what farmers call teddering) up to three days until the hay is perfectly and totally dry. Damp hay rots, and can even become combustible. To store the hay, simply pile it somewhere dry and clean.

Save-a-species: Song thrush

In the UK there has been a severe population decline of the song thrush since the 1970s, and it is now a priority species under the UK Biodiversity Action Plan. A bird of farmland and woodland, it is adept at making itself at home in gardens abundant with invertebrates. A wildflower lawn heaving with worms is an ideal foraging ground.

Song thrushes are similar in size and shape to blackbirds. They have brown upperparts and white breasts dotted with brown spots.

As songsters they rival nightingales. Plant a tree for them to perform from, especially in spring when they proclaim their territory to rivals.

A sure sign of the presence of a song thrush is a stone with fragments of snail shells. They are unique among British birds in using a stone as an 'anvil' to smash mollusc shells.

TOP TEN PLANTS FOR A WILDFLOWER MEADOW OR LAWN

Visit a local wildflower meadow to see which species of wildflower will thrive best in your garden. Here are ten classics. Substitute others according to local climate and soil type.

Yellow rattle *Rhinanthus minor*
Takes its name from the characteristic rattle of the seeds in the purse-like heads in summer. Strictly speaking, *Rhinanthus minor* is a semi-parasite, and, while it can photosynthesise, it is happiest when its roots grasp those of grasses so it can suck the life out of them. In the creation of a wildflower meadow, yellow rattle is as close to indispensable as it gets. As well as controlling the vigour of grasses, yellow rattle produces springtime yellow flowers which are attractive to bees. Once established, never cut yellow rattle between March and July because it will neither bear the experience nor produce seed heads. Cut in July or August, and leave the seed heads on the ground for a day or two for the seeds to fall free. Alternatively, gather the seed heads, then shake over the mown wildflower lawn. If the lawn is scarified before seeding so much the better.

There are six sub-species of yellow rattle. When buying, check with the merchant that your seed is of local provenance.

Cowslip *Primula veris*
Bright yellow and easy to grow, the nectar-rich cowslip flowers in spring, making it an important food source for bees waking from hibernation. Before the Second World War, humans made use of the bobbly cowslip flowers in making wine. This takes an awful lot of cowslip flowers, but if you want to have a taste of the ambrosia the garden's bees are enjoying, the flowers make a pleasant addition to salads.

Field scabious *Knautia arvensis*
To be used on calcareous soils only, field scabious has nectar-laden pink or lilac pin-cushion flowers (June–October) which turn to

seed heads loved by finches and sparrows in autumn and winter. A win-win for wildlife.

Ox-eye daisy *Leucanthemum vulgare*
Such local names for the ox-eye daisy as rising sun and sun daisy are a clue to the flowering period of this member of the chrysanthemum family, which is midsummer. A quick-growing perennial, with an abundance of familiar daisy flowers: bright yellow suns in the centre with a white collar.

Harebell *Campanula rotundifolia*
The dainty, blue flowers of the harebell make it one of the prettiest additions to a wildflower lawn. With a late flowering (July–September), the plant can make an important autumnal source of nectar for a range of bees. Despite its name, it is not foodstuff beloved of hares (or rabbits); the hare of the harebell is a witch's animal. The plant's long association with devilry, fairies and magick is caught in such local names as fairy cap, fairy bell, old man's bell (that is, the Devil's) and witches' thimble. In Scotland, the natives were less superstitious and stuck to no-nonsense description and called it 'bluebell'.

Red clover *Trifolium pratense*
Much loved by gardeners and farmers for fixing nitrogen in the soil, red clover also has bright round purple flower heads that produce prodigious amounts of nectar, hence its local name of bee bread. Like cowslips, red clover is edible for humans too.

Yarrow *Achillea millefolium*
A perennial with creamy white discs and long multi-divided leaves (hence '*millefolium*' or 'thousand leaf') which look like green feather boas. Its flowers are an important source of high summer nectar. There is probably more folklore attached to yarrow than any other plant; by repute Achilles used it to bind the wounds of his

soldiers in the Trojan Wars and the Celts consumed the herb to foresee the future. The leaves also make a pleasant, slightly bitter tea for modern man and woman.

Sorrel *Rumex acetosa*

Sorrel is an upright perennial with arrow-shaped leaves and reddish flowers on slender spikes. These appear in May and June. Reaching heights of 60cm it adds a 'storey' of height to a meadow. Sorrel is from the Old French 'surele', meaning sour, in acknowledgement of the tart taste of its leaves due to their high oxalic acid content.

The rusty-red seeds are an important food source for finches (goldfinches in particular), and the leaves make a meal for the caterpillars of the small copper butterfly.

Bird's-foot trefoil *Lotus corniculatus*

Commonly known as 'bacon and eggs' in honour of its red-and-yellow flowers, *Lotus corniculatus* has other, less engaging names which give an instant mind picture of its seed pods – such as old woman's toe nails and devil's claws.

As tough as boxing gloves (yet another of its seventy or so local names), *Lotus corniculatus* will grow in nearly all soils to produce its nectar-rich blooms. The common blue, the dingy skipper and six-spot burnet are just three of the butterfly and moth species whose larvae eat the leaves. A must-have.

Lady's smock *Cardamine pratensis*

For a spring flower in a damp meadow, look no further than lady's smock. This perennial in the wallflower family reaches 60cm tall on an erect stem; the delicate flowers are pale pink. Also known as cuckoo flower or milkmaids, lady's smock is the primary food plant for the larvae of the orange-tip butterfly.

How to cheat

Try laying wildflower turf, which comes low in nutrients and is supplied in rolls so it can be laid like a normal lawn. Available from specialist suppliers.

Tip: Where soil fertility is too high to permit a traditional, perennial wildflower meadow to flourish, try an annual cornfield meadow of plants such as corn cockle (*Agrostemma githago*), corn marigold (*Glebionis segetum*), corn chamomile (*Anthemis arvensis*) and cornflower (*Centaurea cyanus*). Sowing should be done on bare soil. Additional sowings may be required over the next few years.

WILDLIFE TO WATCH OUT FOR

Grass snake

The grass snake is the largest species of British snake (70–100cm in length), and is identified by its olive-green body and a distinctive yellow-and-black collar behind the head. It is non-venomous; the poisonous adder has a more thick-set body and a distinct zigzag down its back. Adders are rarely found in gardens. Slow worms can be confused with grass snakes, but slow worms (actually a type of non-venomous legless lizard) have a bullet-shaped head and are generally coppery brown in colour.

As their natural habitat is lost, grass snakes are relying increasingly on gardens to forage for food and for nesting. Compost heaps are favourite sites for females to lay eggs, while long grass is their natural hunting territory. Their diet consists mainly of amphibians. Installing a pond will make your garden extra-attractive to the grass snake. Grass snakes rarely bite humans. But do not handle them. The snake has two tactics to dissuade certain predators from killing it. One is to play dead with its tongue hanging out. The other is to release a pungent substance from the anal gland mixed with faecal matter. It is very, very smelly.

Meadow grasshopper

The quintessential grassland insect, notable for its ability to hop and, from June, to chirp. The sound is produced by 'stridulation': the rubbing of body parts together. Meadow grasshoppers rub hind legs against front wings; the male is louder and more persistent than the female. Grasshoppers are an important protein source for a variety of predators.

Green woodpecker

This shy bird nests in old trees yet is largely a ground feeder, and is increasingly tempted to suburban wildlife lawns in search of its favourite food – ants – which it laps up with its long tongue. Listen out for its distinctive call, which sounds like mad laughing.

Bumblebee

These are stout, very hairy bees which are generally black with degrees of yellow markings. Common bumblebees include garden, field, buff-tailed, red-tailed and white-tailed varieties. The furry coats help them keep snug, and they can fly from early morning to late evening, even in drizzle.

Bumblebees will only sting if threatened. They are important pollinators of many plants and fruiting trees. Highly social insects, bumblebees live in a complex colony consisting of a queen, males and sterile worker females. It's the workers who gather pollen and nectar to feed the later batches of grubs. New queens and males hatch at the end of the season and mate. Old queens, males and workers die. The new queens hibernate, and the cycle begins again.

Goldfinch

One of the prettiest of garden birds, with its bright red forehead and bright yellow wing bars, the goldfinch will descend in breezy, chattering groups to eat seed heads in the wildflower lawn from August, nimbly grasping stems as they do so. The collective noun for goldfinches is a 'charm'. And they are charming, with a liquid twittering song that made them favourite cage birds in the past.

Meadow brown

The meadow brown butterfly is on the wing in the summer, from June to September, and flies in dull weather when other butterflies are inactive. A medium-sized butterfly, the meadow brown can be distinguished by orange patches containing one 'eyespot' on the forewings. The caterpillars feed on a variety of grasses such as bents, fescues and meadow-grasses. They do not wander far afield if they can help it and meadow browns mating and flying in the July heat may never leave your garden.

Common shrew/Pygmy shrew

The common shrew is a chocolate brown colour on the back and near white on the underparts. It looks as velvety as a mole, and has a markedly long nose which constantly twitches as it searches for food. The pygmy shrew, the smallest mammal likely to turn up in a garden, looks almost identical. The main distinguishing feature between the two cousins is size, with the common shrew measuring up to 8cm (including tail) and the pygmy 6cm.

They are both more likely to be heard than seen, as they like to hunt invertebrates in the dense cover of long grass and hedge debris; they communicate by high-pitched squeaks. Shrews require gargantuan amounts of food due to a very high metabolic rate, and a shrew can eat its own body weight in twenty-four hours. So they are almost always hunting and eating, day and night, night and day.

Where you have shrews, tawny owls and kestrels – which prey on these energetic, entertaining animals – often follow. Most birds have no sense of smell. Mammalian predators, on the other hand, rarely eat shrews because shrews have glands on their flanks that produce a quite foul odour. Hence Tiddles bringing in shrews as a gift rather than scoffing them herself.

Starling

The starling is yet another once-familiar bird to have suffered decline in recent decades, and it's now on the European Red List. Gaudily iridescent plumage, sparkled with a galaxy of white dots, and a spivy comical manner, mark it from the blackbird for which it is sometimes mistaken. The starling has a dagger of a beak, with special muscles which enable it to open when probed into the ground, all the better to haul earthworms from the grass with. Excellent mimics, starlings can impersonate other birds and car alarms. Their own song is a rambling repertoire of whistles and clicks. Hugely sociable beings, starlings often gather in large flocks or 'murmurations' to roost at night.

As well as pecking over your wildflower lawn for worms and daddy longlegs, among other invertebrates, a starling will devour any suitable food scraps you care to place before it in winter. A nest box high on the wall will also be a help in maintaining numbers of this entertaining rake.

CHAPTER 3
PONDS AND WETLANDS

Ponds are magnets for wildlife. Of all the habitats you can create to aid wildlife in your garden, a pond is the most useful. Any pond is better than no pond, and even a sunken bucket will make a discernible difference to the number and types of animals that visit the garden. Dragonflies are quite content breeding in old washbasins and Mrs Tiggy-Winkle will quite happily slurp from an upturned metal dustbin lid. But as a general rule, the bigger the pond the better: a bigger pond provides a range of complex mini-habitats, and deep water is less likely to boil in high summer or freeze solid in winter. A hibernating frog will thank you for a deep end of about 60–90cm.

Although there are still around 470,000 ponds in the British countryside, many are polluted and degraded by lack of maintenance. Some of the loss of habitat has been offset by the suburban gardener, with roughly 1 in 10 British back gardens now having a pond. A pond in your garden is an individual incremental increase in the freshwater habitat; a series of ponds in a neighbourhood can establish an aquatic corridor that allows wildlife to move around. Ponds also store carbon, helping to reduce global warming. In addition to the wildlife that lives in and around ponds, they're watering holes for passing birds and mammals, from migrating redwings to the neighbourhood badger on his nightly perambulation. Ponds provide endless interest and drama for humans. They also create a place of tranquillity and of beauty in the garden.

STEP-BY-STEP: BUILD A WILDLIFE POND

Depending on size and type, a pond will take a weekend or two to complete. It's best to dig a pond in autumn when the ground is soft, and let it fill naturally with rainwater. If you are installing a pond at any other time of year, try and store rainwater beforehand to fill it – tap water is death to ponds because it often has high levels of nitrogen and phosphorus which encourage 'green pond syndrome', an attack of choking algae.

Step 1. Siting

Where you dig your pond is critical, because a shallow pond in a very sunny site will be prone to algal blooms and drying out. Part shade, part sun is perfect – and this can be easily manufactured by planting tall marginal plants (plants of the edge or 'margin') such as yellow flag (*Iris pseudacorus*). Tadpoles adore bathing in shallow, well-lit warm water; as adult frogs they prefer lurking in moist shade. And you will want frogs in your pond.

Your pond may need topping up with water; the easiest way to accomplish this is to connect a hose to the overflow of a water butt and – hey presto! – the pond will fill automatically during rainy days. So make sure to position it within reach of a natural water supply. Conversely, do not position a pond where it will receive 'run off' from a road or a chemically laden lawn.

Step 2. Choosing a liner

Unless you live in an area of heavy clay, your pond will need a liner. For small ponds, a glass fibre or moulded pool can be used. Their disadvantage is the limited range of shapes on offer, and their tendency to have sides too steep for wildlife.

A flexible liner of butyl rubber or heavy-duty stabilised PVC is the other option; received opinion always plumps for butyl rubber but the latest heavy-duty stabilised PVC is comparable. And cheaper. The great advantage of a flexible liner is that the pond can be landscaped to suit your and your wildlife's dreams. Flexible liners, however, are fiddlier to fit.

Step 3. Design

The minimum size for a pond is 4–5m², and it should combine deep water and shallows.

At least two sides of the pond should be gently sloping up to finish in a broad shallow zone. The greatest variety of plants and animals live in shallow water at the edge, often of just 2–5cm depth. Shallows also provide a bathing area for birds.

The deepest part of the pond need not be at the end; the centre is fine. A depth of 90cm will do more than lure male frogs for hibernation; it creates ideal swimming conditions for great crested newts.

Create planting shelves – ledges of about 25cm in width, 10–20cm under the eventual surface of the water. Alternatively you can make ledges later by stacking rocks and stones.

When designing your own pond remember that a curved or kidney shape looks natural, and is easier to fit a flexible liner into than an angled shape.

Tip: To calculate the amount of pond liner you will need for your pond, use this equation:

(length + 2 depths + 30cm) by (width + 2 depths + 30cm)

Example: for a pond with the final dimensions of 5m long, 2.5m wide and 0.5m deep:

$$(5 + (2 \times 0.5) + 0.3) \text{ by } (2.5 + (2 \times 0.5) + 0.3) =$$
liner dimensions of 6.3m x 3.8m

The equation allows for an excess to anchor the liner around the edge of the pond.

Step 4. Excavation

Mark out the shape of the pond with a hose or rope. With a pre-fab pond, simply invert it in the right location and 'trace' around the edge with the hose.

Unless you are fit or have willing helpers, hire a mini-digger at this point. They are fun, and faster at digging than moles and badgers. Whether using machinery or manpower, dig the deepest areas first before establishing the slopes and planting shelves.

Use the barrow loads of top soil you are suddenly presented with to make a bank behind the pond or to create a raised bed elsewhere in the garden.

Step 5. Fitting a liner

To avoid puncturing the liner, pre-line the bottom and sides of your pond with unwanted woollen blankets or 3cm of fine builder's sand.

Choose a windless day for fitting, and have a large pair of scissors handy. Take the liner to one end and unroll it across the pond, making sure there is excess all the way round. Don't drag the liner when fitting, as any overlooked protruding stones will rip it. Put some bricks on each corner to weigh the liner down.

This is also the time to build ledges from stone and rock, if you haven't 'profiled' these in (created them when cutting away the soil). To provide an extra cushion under the stones, use hessian sacks or cut spare liner in the shape of the ledge. Put this in position and pile up to the desired height with large stones.

Now fill your pond with rainwater from a butt or two, or perhaps the rain will simply pour down on cue. The water will press the liner into shape, smoothing out creases and pleats as they arise.

Once the pond is nearly full, cut the edge of the liner leaving a 30cm overlap all round. To bury the edge of the liner, either: cut horizontally into the surrounding turf and tuck the liner underneath the lifted turf (you may need to stand in the pond to do this) or pile materials such as pebbles, logs, rocks or paving slabs on top of the liner edge. Concrete slabs have the added advantage of providing a 'hard standing' for a human viewing point. Then fill to the brim.

You now have a garden pond! Do not fret about the ugliness of the visible parts of the liner. A covering of a chemically inert substrate – washed gravel or children's play sand are ideal – will both hide the liner and provide footing for plants. Do not be tempted to use the soil from the hole as a base for pond plants since it will be too nutrient rich. Time and algae will also cover the liner up.

STOCKING THE POND WITH PLANTS

A new pond will eventually become colonised by plants without human intervention. But few pond-makers can bear to see their pond naked, so a trip to the garden centre or a specialist water nursery is almost certain. Always stock with native plant species. Most British pond plants are quite tough and can be introduced at any time of year. Some are rampant, and you may wish to plant them in the specialist plastic baskets or terracotta pots.

Correctly chosen plants will keep the water clean without the need for costly electrical equipment. And with the right plants you will also have a habitat for an abundance of pond creatures. Almost all pond fauna need the sanctuary of dense vegetation, especially in the shallows. In other parts of the pond try and introduce a selection of submerged and floating plants to create a diverse range of underwater worlds.

Tip: Put a seat by the pond so you can comfortably enjoy watching all the dramas of pond life. A mini dry stone wall or a large log provide both seating for the human rear and an abode for beasties.

TOP TEN PLANTS FOR A POND

If you have filled your pond with tap water let it 'stand' for a couple of days before planting. These enables some of the chemicals in the water to break down.

Marginals

These are pondside plants that grow at the shallow edges of a pond, and often extend over land and water. Plant them in 2–5cm of water. They provide perches and food for hoverflies and bees, as well as safety for swimming beasts.

Marsh marigold *Caltha palustris*

Produces bright yellow flowers early in spring, just as the first bees and other insects are emerging. Also known as kingcup. Spreads by creeping stalks and seeds, and is undemanding; moisture is all it requires. Grows up to 60cm in height, and its dense foliage provides necessary shadowy shelter for insects and amphibians. A must-have in a wetland wildlife garden.

Yellow flag *Iris pseudacorus*

Grows to 2m in height, and in summer produces yellow blooms highly prized by bees and hoverflies. Will grow in a bog or in water up to 15cm deep; in the latter context dragonfly larvae use its leaves as ladders out of the water as well as a place for pupation. The density of the foliage offers myriad possibilities for wildlife to hide in. Iris sawfly larvae eat the leaves.

Water forget-me-not *Myosotis palustris*

Makes a mirage of small yellow-eyed, powder-blue flowers in summer, which are much visited by butterflies, bees and bumblebees. A herbaceous perennial whose mounds of leaves provide dense cover for froglets and small invertebrates. The minute seeds are foodstuff for finches.

Watercress *Rorippa nasturtium-aquaticum*
Grows quickly, and has the added advantage that, if it needs to be hacked back, you can eat the cuttings. Wash well. Safest 'souped'.

Also consider: marsh pennywort (*Hydrocotyle vulgaris*), marsh cinquefoil (*Comarum palustre*), water dock (*Rumex hydrolapathum*), lesser spearwort (*Ranunculus flammula*).

Oxygenators

These are plants that live entirely or almost entirely underwater. Unfortunately most native oxygenators are intolerant of pollution, but the following submerged aquatic plants are all relatively robust. Oxygenators are important in the control of algae and duckweed.

Water milfoil *Myriophyllum spicatum*
Newts like to lay eggs under its spiked leaves. A good oxygenator.

Broad-leaved pondweed *Potamogeton natans*
Easy to establish, and much favoured by invertebrates.

Hornwort *Ceratophyllum demersum*
An underwater jungle beloved of all pond creatures.

Emergent plants

These have erect stems and leaves. As well as providing interesting natural architecture they provide a ladder for dragonfly nymphs to crawl up preparatory to adulthood.

Bulrush *Typha latifolia*
Also known as reed mace, this is a vigorous perennial, which grows to over 2m in height. To keep under control you may need to cut vigorously.

Bog bean *Menyanthes trifoliata*
A delightful little plant which produces spikes of delicate pink flowers.

33

Also consider: greater pond sedge (*Carex riparia*), soft rush (*Juncus effuses*), branched bur-reed (*Sparganium erectum*).

Floating plants

These can be free-floating or have trailing roots, but all have leaves that float on the surface. The leaves provide beds for all manner of aquatic insects to mate on, as well as cooling shade for invertebrates in the water below. They also help stop algae build-up.

White waterlily *Nymphaea alba*

To be favoured over the yellow water lily (*Nuphar lutea*), which has absolutely outsize leaves and an odd alcohol smell. The exquisite linen-white flowers of *Nymphaea alba* are visited by countless species of butterfly and insect. You may need to control the lily by planting it in terracotta pots.

Also consider: amphibious bistort (*Persicaria amphibian*).

Tip: Your pond will become even more of a wildlife wonder if you plant native flowers adjacent to it. These will provide a foraging area for amphibians, and aquatic insects, such as hoverflies, will seek out the flowers' nectar. Try devil's-bit scabious (*Succisa pratensis*), teasel (*Dipsacus fullonum*), hemp agrimony (*Eupatorium cannabinum*) and red valerian (*Centranthus ruber*). Cow parsley (*Anthriscus sylvestris*) provides excellent landing pads for hoverflies. At the very least, let the grass near the pond grow tall. This will provide a welcome, if rather mundane-looking, habitat for many creatures.

PLANTS TO AVOID

Some invasive, non-native species will take over your pond, if given the chance. They can also escape into the wild and cause environmental mayhem by blocking waterways and appropriating the habitat of native plants. Their removal is expensive on the public purse – about £200 million is spent annually on removing non-native weeds. So, **do not** stock your pond with:

- Floating pennywort *Hydrocotyle ranunculoides*
- Parrot feather *Myriophyllum aquaticum*
- Water fern *Azolla filiculoides*
- New Zealand pigmyweed/Australian swamp-stonecrop *Crasula helmsii*
- Water hyacinth *Eichornia crassipes*
- Water lettuce *Pistia stratiotes*
- Water primrose *Ludwigia grandiflora*

Save-a-species: Common toad

Mr and Mrs Common Toad are not as common as they used to be. Or as common as their name suggests. The common toad is now considered a priority species under the Biodiversity Action Plan.

As well as pesticides and habitat destruction taking their toll, toads are killed in significant numbers every March by cars as the amphibians waddle across the road to their ancestral breeding pools. Once in the pond, the male toads mate with considerable vigour (and as fish, stones and other males can bear witness, not a great deal of discrimination). Spring is the only season when toads live in water. (George Orwell thought toads mating the sure sign that spring had come in 'Some Thoughts on the Common Toad'.)

Toads' eggs are easily identified. Instead of the dense clumps of spawn laid by frogs, toadspawn is laid out in strings containing a double or triple row of eggs (a single row of eggs would indicate the rare natterjack toad). Tadpoles, which usually hatch around March, then become toadlets and leave the pond by the end of July.

Common toads are most active at night when they hunt their favourite foods. They feed on any moving prey they can swallow, which are generally invertebrates. This makes them useful in the garden when it comes to controlling populations of pest animals such as slugs and snails. Usually toads patiently sit and await their prey, which they catch with their long tongues, although they will roam if necessary.

When temperatures drop in the autumn, they will start to look for a suitable spot for hibernation. You can encourage toads to stay in the garden by providing a Toad Hall in the shape of a log pile, rock pile or an old flower pot at the bottom of the hedge. Pack plenty of leaf litter round it.

Take care in autumn and winter before setting bonfires alight. Toads quite often hibernate in their lower depths.

Both adult and tadpole toads emit a toxin (bufotoxin) from their skin to deter predators; it is known to cause irritation in humans. Toads should only be handled with gloves.

POND MANAGEMENT

To keep the sort of pond you will doubtless have in mind at creation – clear water full of beetles, snails, newts, dragonflies, with a bat circling overhead on a late summer's eve – requires some maintenance. Luckily, select the rights plants and three-quarters of the job is done for you. The other quarter you have to do.

SPRING

As soon as duckweed (*Lemnaceae*) appears, rake or pull it off by hand.

New plants grow quickly in the warming water, so plant any friendly native species now. A planting rate of 1–3 per m² will usually provide excellent cover in a year. Otherwise, sit back and enjoy the amphibian mating and egg-laying season.

SUMMER

People often panic if their pond starts drying out in the summer. Don't. Levels can dip dramatically without any negative results, and even drying up is unlikely to be a disaster. Annual drying out of ponds has been going on for millennia, and there are even species that thrive on the process. Some of Britain's most interesting water bodies are the temporary ponds of the New Forest, home to the fairy shrimp which is specially adapted for the drying-out process. A pond gone to desert will quickly recolonise when the water naturally returns.

Indeed, since dragonflies lay their eggs around exposed pond margins, it's best not to keep the pond topped up to the brim in summer.

Overheating may be a problem in shallow ponds still resplendent with tadpoles. If the water temperature goes above 35 degrees, tadpoles will die, so add rainwater little and often – remember that a sudden flood of cold water will reduce the temperature of the pond, and consequently the body temperature of the amphibians in it. The shock can kill them.

Tip: Blanket weed and green algae tend to be a problem in new ponds, dredged ponds, those positioned in direct sunlight and those filled from the mains water supply. The cause is the 'richness' of the water. In summer, remove blanket weed and algae by hand or with a rake. Algal blooms are usually short lived, and the pond should settle down as zooplankton increase and eat the algae.

Reduce the level of nutrients in the water to control persistent infestations by removing bottom sediment in winter (see below). Planting shade-casting flora species will also help. A quick fix may be had by putting a bale of barley straw into the pond. As the straw rots it releases chemicals that kill the algae; when it has turned black, about six months later, remove it. Unless the cause of the problem is addressed you will need to repeat the barley straw prescription.

AUTUMN

You will find that some plants multiply with unnerving ferocity. Be brutal with species bent on pond domination by pulling them up every year and reducing their presence by a good third. Do the job in autumn so as not to disturb breeding or hibernating animals. Aim always to keep at least 30 per cent of the pond surface open water.

Remember to leave the discarded vegetation by the pond's side for a day or two so that bugs and amphibians can escape back to the pond. After that, chuck it on the compost heap.

Over time, the inevitable build up of fallen leaves and dead vegetation at the bottom of the pond may turn the water brown, as all the available oxygen will be taken up by the process of decay. A layer of silt accumulates, which is no bad thing in itself as it is useful for hibernating frogs; eventually, however, the pond will become shallower and shallower ... until it becomes a muddy hollow. In a small pond, you will need to dredge every five years or so; in a large pond every ten years. Again, this is a smelly task for autumn, before hibernation begins. For a small pond, silt can be removed with a bucket, for a large pond, a sludge vacuum or pump may be required. These can be hired from aquatic centres.

The dredged sludge can safely be added to flower borders.

Tip: It's a good idea to cover your pond with netting during the autumn to prevent it from filling up with fallen leaves. Be sure to leave some of the surface free for wildlife access.

WINTER

Since amphibians will hopefully be hibernating in the bottom of your pond, it must not freeze solid. Ponds deeper than 60cm seldom suffer, but for shallower ponds remember a frog in stasis can tolerate low oxygen levels, but it cannot survive *no* oxygen levels. A simple solution is a tennis ball floating on the top of the pond, which should prevent a great freeze over. Never use boiling water to break the ice; positioning a saucepan of hot water on the surface until the ice has melted sufficiently is safer for the pond's denizens.

POND LIFE TO WATCH OUT FOR

There is no need to 'add' animals to the pond; they will find their own way. (The exception is fish, but you really don't want these because they will eat all the other animals.) All you need to do is keep the grass and vegetation long at the edge of the pond, and provide a log pile or rock pile as a shelter for hibernation. Dragonflies are among the quickest colonisers, and are usually present in all medium-sized ponds with good water quality. A whole range of fauna will inadvertently be deposited by birds, including snails. Be aware that in transferring amphibians from another pond you may also be transferring pathogens.

Pond skaters
Also known as water striders, these are dull-coloured fast-moving bugs (between 0.8 and 1.8cm in length) that walk on top of the

water using their splayed long middle and rear legs; the front legs are short and used for grasping prey. The variety most likely to be found in a garden pond is the common pond skater. Ripple-sensitive hairs on the legs locate struggling prey on the surface, to which the skaters dart along the surface film, then ferociously stab it with their mouth parts.

Whirligig beetle

A quite comical small black beetle, that takes its name from its habit of frantically whirling round and round on the water's surface when alarmed. The eyes are in two parts, enabling it to see up and down simultaneously. Like the water boatman, the whirligig can trap air against its body for long swims. A strong flyer, and often the first bug to colonise a new pond.

Common backswimmer

Don't be fooled by *Notonecta X galuca*'s small size or idiosyncratic habit of swimming upside-down. This wedge-shaped bug is the monster of the pond.

The backswimmer hangs from the surface film until it detects the vibrations of prey moving about. Then the backswimmer dives down at dazzling speed, clutches the prey with its forelegs, stabs it with its feeding beak (rostrum), before injecting a toxic juice to paralyse and liquefy, much as spiders do. The deadly deed done, the backswimmer takes a leisurely swim while sucking out the 'soupy' innards of its victim. Lunch is often bigger, much bigger than the 1.6cm backswimmer. A minnow fish, for instance.

From above, the lurking backswimmer often has the appearance of a mercury blob due to its holding of an air bubble on its chest. The beast can live for nearly a year. Mating is in spring.

They fly well, too.

You can be assured the backswimmer will visit your pond.

Common or lesser water boatman

An aquatic herbivorous bug about 1cm long, with oar-like hind legs, and a back patterned with black and yellow, which really does seem to row about underwater. Unlike the backswimmer (above), the boatman swims the right way up.

The boatman possesses two extraordinary tricks. Firstly, it can scuba dive – by coming to the surface, collecting a bubble of air under its wings and then descending again. Secondly, males make music by rubbing their front legs against a ridge on their heads. This stridulating makes an underwater chirping song much like that made by terranean crickets and grasshoppers, and is intended to woo the girls.

One species of boatman found in Britain (and maybe in your pond), the 2mm-long lesser water boatman is, size for size, the loudest animal on earth. By stridulating with its penis down in the murky deep, *Micronecta scholtzi* can bang out 99.2 decibels, and is quite audible to humans on the pond's banks.

Dragonflies and damselflies

These slender flying insects – country people used to call them 'devil's darning needles' – make up the scientific order *Odonata*, with damselflies being the sub-order *Zygoptera* and dragonflies the sub-order *Anisoptera*. With their extraordinarily brilliant colouration, they are flying jewels of the British natural world, rivalling kingfishers in their exoticism. Damselflies and dragonflies are very closely related to each other, but generally damselflies are smaller and always rest with their wings closed lengthways against their bodies (dragonflies rest with wings outspread). Largely unchanged in appearance since pre-historic times, both sub-orders share a mating method requiring *Kama Sutra* dexterity. When interlocked, the two insects form a seamless 'wheel' or 'heart' shape. Depending on the species, mating takes place on the wing, perched on vegetation or the ground.

Dragonflies and damselflies are marvels of aeronautic engineering. The angle and beat of their four wings can be controlled independently, which allows dragonflies to fly up, down, sideways or backwards and hover for up to a minute. Some dragonflies can reach speeds in excess of 30mph. Voracious predators, the adults locate their flying meal by use of their outsize eyes, which can see in almost all directions at once. The similarly carnivorous larvae (nymphs) are aquatic, sometimes for years, scuttling round their watery home by means of water squirted from the anus. When they catch their prey, which can be tadpole-sized, the nymphs suck the juices out to leave a hollow shell or skin.

There are about thirty-six species of the sub-order *Anisoptera* in Britain, of which the 70mm southern hawker dragonfly is a regular breeder in garden ponds. Southern hawkers breed in late summer, with mating taking up to an hour, after which the female saws a hole in plants or rotten wood in or next to the pond into which her eggs are deposited. They are inquisitive insects, and often fly close to investigate humans. They are harmless.

Other species of dragonfly frequently recorded on garden ponds are the common darter, the four-spotted chaser, the broad-bodied chaser and the emperor. The blue-tailed damselfly is a stalwart coloniser of ponds, with the large red and the azure not far behind.

Water hoglouse
Dig around in the bottom of the pond and you are likely to turn up the splendidly named water hoglouse, which for all scientific intents and purposes is an aquatic woodlouse. They are remarkably able to tolerate low oxygen levels, and will consequently tolerate mild pollution. They breathe through gills at the rear of their abdomen. Also known as the common water slater.

Common frog

Although active both day and night, the common frog prefers to hunt in the darkness; a true gardener's friend, its diet largely consists of insects, slugs, snails and worms. During spring, males purr to attract a mate, as sure a sign of lengthening days as the arrival of the cuckoo. The jelly-like fertilised eggs, frogspawn, are laid between February and April and hatch into tadpoles which change over a period of between twelve and fourteen weeks into froglets. The common frog may live for a surprisingly long time, with eight years of life being unremarkable. During winter, frogs can hibernate under water as they possess the ability to breathe through their skin as well as through their lungs. Frogs can also change colour to suit their surroundings, though they usually dress in grey-green. Widespread across Britain.

Tip: To tell the difference between the common frog and the common toad:
- When disturbed, frogs tend to hop, toads tend to crawl.
- Frogs have smooth skin, toads have warty skin.
- Frogs have black patches behind the eye, toads have large lumps (parotoid glands) behind the eye.

Common newt

Britain possesses three species of newt – the palmate newt, the great crested newt and the common or smooth newt. The latter is the likeliest visitor to the garden ponds of Britain.

Common newts are olive green or pale brown with a bright orange, black-spotted underside. In the breeding season, the male sports a wavy crest from head to tail. They may reach 11cm in length, with the male slightly larger than the female. Their average lifespan is six years. They are nocturnal and spend the day hiding under large logs or stones.

From mid-October the newts hibernate, emerging again in February or March. Males seek out females and entice them by wafting a glandular secretion and shaking their tails. The male drops a packet of sperm near the female, which she collects. A week or so later she lays up to twelve eggs per day on underwater leaves, which she folds over into a protective parcel. The larvae hatch after a fortnight or so, and during the next ten weeks change into juvenile newts, a metamorphosis similar to that of the larvae of the toad and frog. A young adult newt is known as an eft. The efts leave the water to hunt on land, and share the same carnivorous diet of slugs, worms and insects as the landlubber adult newts.

Outside the breeding season you'll find the common newt far away from water, in woods, parks and farmland.

Some people mistake newts for lizards. Although they look similar, they are quite different, with lizards being land creatures and newts being true amphibians who spend part of their year in water. Lizard skin is dry and scaly, whereas newt skin (which common newts shed once a week) is moist, velvety and seemingly scale-less.

A common newt can be told apart from a palmate newt, which is a similar species, by the presence of dark spots on the underside of the throat and the absence of a black mask around the eyes. The great crested newt is on an altogether bigger scale (hence the 'great'), with adults reaching 17cm, and possesses markedly lumpy skin which accounts for its colloquial name of warty newt. The great crested newt is an endangered species, one of twenty-two animals and plants on the European Red List. They can live as long as twenty-seven years.

Tip: When food at the birth pond becomes scarce, young newts wander in search of new hunting territories. If you have a garden pond which is yet to be colonised by newts, place log piles by the side of the water. Logs are five-star accommodation for newts because they create a damp micro-habitat with teeming supplies of insects for the amphibians to feast on. Carefully roll back a log next to a pond with good water and you are very likely to find a dozing newt underneath. Don't disturb them in winter though, as they need to stay warm.

POND DIPPING

A net and a jam jar or shallow white oven dish are all that is needed for pond dipping. Generations of children, not having a net handy, have made do by taking the foot and ankle from a pair of tights, using a wire coat hanger to make the net's mouth and sticking it into the end of a bamboo cane. You can also use a kitchen sieve.

- Move your small-gauge net slowly through the pond.
- To identify your haul, either tip contents into a jam jar or, better still, a white dish. The white background is ideal to spot mini-beasties against.
- Try not to handle pond animals, not least because some of them bite. The apparently insignificant backswimmer has jabbing mouth parts that can pierce human skin. Painfully so.
- Identify with a photographic guide.
- Putting a drop of pond water under a microscope will open up a whole universe …
- Don't forget to gently put back the animals as soon as possible. They can quickly become overheated or use up all the oxygen in the water.

MAKE A MINI-POND

If you only have a small garden, pretty much any waterproof container will make a mini-pond. Wooden half-tubs and old stone sinks work well, or else choose a metal bucket or a glazed ceramic pot. Neither do ponds have to be 'dug in'. If your pond is free-standing, just make sure there is a ramp in and out (stones, bricks and plants are ideal) so that wildlife has access. Newts and frogs will sometimes lay their eggs in a pond only a metre square, and if they can't be tempted to breed in your container pond, it can still help them keep cool in summer. Many other creatures will make use of it.

- Fill your container with rainwater. If you have to use tap water, leave it to stand for a couple of days to neutralise.
- Select your plants. As with a bigger pond, choose a combination of marginals, oxygenators and floating aquatics. Try water soldier (*Stratiotes aloides*) as an oxygenator, and dwarf lily (*Nymphaea odorata*) as a deep water aquatic. One lily will be enough for a container pond.
- Plant any marginals in plastic aquatic baskets lined with gravel, filled with a specially designed compost (or clay loam) and dressed with gravel. To get the right height for the plant use bricks, placing the planted basket on top.

Containers can also be used to spread and increase the wetland habitat around larger gardens. The more ponds the merrier.

Water safety

Rather fewer children drown in ponds than our imagination would have us believe, but why take risks?
- Always supervise young children near a pond.
- Talk (calmly!) to children about the dangers of water; you want them to be aware but not petrified.

- Wash hands after pond dipping.
- A pond in a corner can be attractively fenced off to keep toddlers out while still letting most wildlife in. Think American-style picket fencing.
- If a pond is absolutely out of the question because of child safety, consider a bog garden.

BOG GARDEN

Do not let the uninspiring name put you off. A bog garden can be a garden feature of unusual, strange beauty. For amphibians it is very close to heaven.

A bog is a mimicked marsh. Since the bog garden consists of permanently waterlogged soil, and invariably requires a PVC or butyl liner, it is usually made at the same time as the pond to which it is the natural sidekick.

If you are constructing your bog simultaneously with your pond, excavate the shallow bog area to the side of the pond – but leave a small bank between the two. The bog should be no more than 45cm deep and with very shallow sides. Think saucer. When you install the liner in the pond let the relevant edge overlap the bank and flow down into the bog hollow and up the far side. The idea is to let the water of the pond slightly lap over the bank – by approximately 5cm – and into the bog area. Secure the liner on the bog edge with stones or by tucking it into the turf. Pile stones on the dividing bank so the water from the pond can seep through into the bog.

Puncture the bog liner with a fork; water needs to drain out. You are creating a marsh not a swamp.

Unlike a pond, a bog needs nutrient-rich soil. Add manure or leaf litter to the excavated soil and refill. Leave for a week before planting.

STEP-BY-STEP: MAKE A STAND-ALONE BOG GARDEN

Since a stand-alone bog garden will not be kept moist by a pond, it needs to be positioned somewhere you can run rainwater to it or you can adapt an existing damp and soggy area of the garden.

Step 1. Dig a saucer shape no more than 45cm deep to whatever breadth takes your fancy or space allows. The word 'bog' is hardly inspiring and most people dig their garden wetland out of a sense of resigned duty. True, the bog will not be a riot of colour in mid-winter but in spring and summer it should burst with flowers. You will be pleasantly surprised by how lovely you find your bog, and wish it was bigger.

Step 2. With a bog, you do not need to worry about buying expensive liner. PVC will do, so will rubble sacks at a pinch. As with the pondside version of the bog, you need to puncture the liner with a fork.

Step 3. Irrigation is the preferable manner of keeping a bog wet. Take a length of hose, stop up one end and pepper the rest of the hose with holes. The hose needs to be long enough to go across the bottom of the bog, side to side, with 5cm popping up above the ground. Lay the prepared hose in the bottom of the bog, and cover with pebbles or coarse gravel to stop the holes getting bunged up. Put a connector on the exposed hose end. When necessary, the irrigation hose can then be attached to a water butt or tap via another hose.

Step 4. Now fill the bog hole with soil, plus manure or compost: the more of these the merrier.

Step 5. Water thoroughly. Try to use rainwater. If tap water is the only means of soaking the bog, let it stand for several days for the additives to break down.

Step 6. Leave the bog for a week to settle before planting.

Step 7. When you have planted up, cover any bare soil with a 5cm mulch of composted bark or rotted leaves to keep the moisture in.

Tip: If you are making your bog garden on a lawn, place the removed turfs in the bog upside down. They are nutrient-rich, and inverting them will stop the grass from re-growing and colonising the bog.

TOP TEN BOG GARDEN PLANTS

All the pond marginals can be planted in the bog. Here are some other suggestions.

Purple loosestrife *Lythrum salicaria*

Bears tall spikes of bee-loved purple flowers between midsummer and autumn, while the leaves are host to the caterpillars of hawk-moths. The dead foliage will be a winter home to beneficial insects.

Round-leaved sundew *Drosera rotundifolia*

One of Britain's three native carnivorous plants. Children find it endlessly fascinating, but not as fascinating as adults do. Or, indeed, insects. Each leaf has glistening tendrils, which attract insects that get caught on the tendrils' stickiness. The leaf curls around the prey, and the insect is duly eaten.

Meadowsweet *Filipendula ulmaria*

Once a common sight in the old British countryside, *Filipendula ulmaria* has disappeared along with the water meadows that were its main home. The midsummer flowers are indeed sweet to smell (with a hint of almond), and attract many insects. They also make a fine beer. Small seeds appear in autumn and are consumed by mini-mammals and birds. The plant grows up to 90cm in height.

Brooklime *Veronica beccabunga*

A creeping, bright-green plant that produces small blue, white-eyed flowers for months on end, making it a long-serving provider of pollen. Edible by humans, and once given to sailors to combat scurvy.

Water mint *Mentha aquatica*

Beware: like most mints *Mentha aquatica* has hegemonic tendencies. Butterflies and bees enjoy the flowers. You will delight in its refreshing scent. The leaves are host to the larvae of, among other moths: knot grass, water ermine, *Phalonida manniana*, *Pyrausta purpuralis* and *Pyrausta aurata*.

Ragged robin *Lychnis flos-cuculi*

Borne from late spring to early summer, the deeply divided ('ragged') pink flowers are a rich source of nectar, and the preceding buds are consumed by caterpillars of the campion moth. Best grown in full sun.

Marsh woundwort *Stachys palustris*

Produces pinkish-purple flowers, which remain on the plant until winter. Valuable as a nectar source for insects, and a foodstuff for the fascinating green tortoise beetle, which when attacked by predatory insects hunkers down and grips the leaf surface, thus presenting no purchase for the predator.

Bilberry *Vaccinium myrtillus*

Low-growing shrub which favours acidic soils. Also known as whinberry, blaeberry and whortleberry (to list just several of its local names). Produces an edible flat-topped blue berry in summer. The plant is an important food source for numerous butterflies, as well as the bilberry bumblebee.

Hemp agrimony *Eupatorium cannabinum*

A herbaceous perennial which produces a mass of raspberry-and-cream flowers in late summer. These teem ceaselessly with insects, notably brown hairstreak, red admiral, peacock, meadow brown, gatekeeper and small tortoiseshell butterflies. Grows to 2m high, so not advisable for small spaces.

Water avens *Geum rivale*

Also goes by the local name of granny's cap, which gives a useful impression of the charming purple pendant flowers produced by this herbaceous perennial. Good for bees, and if planted in sufficient numbers will produce cover for amphibians. Try the cultivar 'Leonard's Variety'. Will also grow well in moisture-retentive cottage-style borders and wildflower meadows.

> **Tip:** Place stepping stones across a large bog garden for access. The stones will also be used by song thrushes to crack open snail shells.

DO-IN-AN-HOUR: A MINI-BOG

Like a mini-pond, a small bog can quickly be made from any suitable container, from buckets to sinks. Bung up any holes. Half wooden tubs planted up with dwarf bog plants are particularly fetching on patios. Position away from direct sunlight. A container bog will need to be watched carefully over summer to ensure it does not become desiccated by the sun. Moisten when necessary.

Water conservation

With water an increasingly scarce (and costly) resource it makes sense to conserve it. A few simple measures will make a difference to the planet, your pocket and the garden's wildlife. Although some species will survive a drought, most will not thrive. A well-watered garden is a garden with invertebrates near the surface, and in easy scoffing reach for carnivorous birds and mammals. Evaporation

51

from the soil can be achieved by introducing groundcover plants such as yellow archangel (*Lamiastrum galeobdolon*), dead-nettle (*Lamium maculatum*) and bugle (*Ajuga reptans*), or by spreading a mulch of leaf litter, coir, bark chippings or grass cuttings. Tallish plants by the side of a pond or bog garden will provide shade and so reduce drying out. Purple loosestrife is made by nature for this job. To stop run-off during wet periods, try terracing slopes.

Maximise the amount of rainwater you capture by installing butts to take the rain off the shed, garage and greenhouse roof, as well the house. Prop the butt on bricks or blocks so you can get the watering can underneath. Then there is 'grey water' – the domestic waste water from washing bodies, clothes and dishes. If you use an eco-friendly soap or shampoo, and don't use bleach, there is no reason not to put it on the garden. Ladling it into a watering can is the keep-fit option; otherwise, fit piping or polythene tubing over the end of the waste pipe and let it run on to the garden by virtue of gravity.

Always water the garden early in the morning or late in the evening. Hot sun, as well as causing evaporation, will literally boil water-covered plants.

CHAPTER 4
BORDERS

Although flower borders are not natural habitats, they can be vitally valuable for wildlife. They provide food and cover for countless fauna, among them pollinators that are crucial to the entire eco-system. A flower border can also be a reserve for wildflowers that are becoming rare in their natural habitat, the countryside. Besides, flowers look and smell wonderful. Who is not cheered by the sight of a snowdrop in winter or transported into ecstasy by the smell of night-scented stocks on a summer's eve?

While native species should have priority, do not turn your nose up at non-natives that pump out nectar and draw in clouds of insects. Close on their heels will be spotted flycatchers, common frogs and other animals. The butterfly bush (*Buddleia davidii*) hails from China, yet it is one of the indispensables in the wildlife gardens of Great Britain.

To increase the wildlife potential of the border have 'planting zones', or different heights of plants, because this gives an overall greater surface area as well as different micro-habitats. Luckily what looks good to the gardener looks good to a bee or bird. In general, try to have herbaceous perennials at the front, then small flowering shrubs and, if you have space at the back, tall shrubs or small trees.

Tip: Regularly dead-heading your plants will keep the flowers coming – and the wildlife.

A BEE BORDER

Bees are nature's great pollinators, and without them many plant species would become extinct. Pollen becomes stuck to the bee's body when it visits a flower in search of nectar and pollen for food. Then, when the bee moves to another flower of the same species, some of the pollen is transferred to the stigma, the female part of the flower, allowing fertilisation to take place. The plant is then able to set seeds. This process of pollination is essential for many flowering plants, together with nearly all garden fruit trees.

A world without buzzing, enchanting bees would not only be a charmless place, it would be a hungry one. Unfortunately, many species of bee have declined; in Britain alone, two of the twenty-four native species of bumblebee have become extinct. Agricultural pesticides and the destruction of wildflower meadows are implicated in this loss. Fortunately, gardeners can help reverse the dismal decline of the British bee by growing suitable plants in a bee border.

DESIGNING A BEE BORDER

Bees forage for a wide range of flowers, largely because different bee species have different requirements due to shape, habits and genetics. A bee border does not need to be massive; the trick is to plant flowers suitable for short-tongued bees and for long-tongued ones. The chosen collection of plants should also flower – and so feed the bees – for as much of the year as possible. Early nectar-rich plants, for instance, are vital for female bees emerging from hibernation; bumblebee queens in particular need enough food to lay and hatch the first brood of workers.

Generally, modern cultivars, especially those with double or multi flowers, should be avoided because they are so removed from ancestral forms that bees have trouble foraging from them. Some even lack nectar and pollen.

If pesticide must be used in the garden, spray in the evening when bees are less active.

> **Tip:** Flowers in clumps or 'drifts' in sunny places are more useful to bees than single flowers in shady places. The flight of the bee requires huge amounts of energy.

FLOWERS FOR A BEE BORDER: SEASON-BY-SEASON

Key: Bi = biennial; H = herbaceous perennial; S = shrub; C = climber; B = bulbs and corms; A = annual; T = tree

Spring

March–May
Armenian grape hyacinth *Muscari armeniacum* B
Aubretia *Aubrieta deltoidea* H
Blackcurrant *Ribes nigrum* S
Blackthorn or Sloe *Prunus spinosa* S
Bluebell *Hyancinthiodes non-scripta* B
Box *Buxus sempervirens* S
Bugle *Ajuga reptans* H
Cherry *Cornus mas cornelian* T
Crocus (various) *Crocus* spp. & cultivars B
Currant, red/white *Ribes rubrum/Ribes glandulosum* S
Darwin's barberry *Berberis darwinii* S
Dusky cranesbill *Geranium phaeum* H
Flowering cherry *Prunus tenella* S
Flowering currant *Ribes sanguineum* S
Goat willow, pussy willow, male form, not female *Salix caprea* S or T
Gold-dust alyssum *Aurinia saxatilis* H

Gorse *Ulex europaeus* S
Hawthorn *Crataegus monogyna* S or T
Hazel *Corylus avellana* S or T
Hebe *Hebe* spp. & cultivars S
Honesty *Lunaria annua* Bi
Japanese barberry *Berberis thunbergii* S
Japanese quince *Chaenomeles speciosa* S
Judas tree *Cercis siliquastrum* T
Juniper-leaved thrift *Armeria juniperifolia* H
Lenten rose, hybrid *Helleborus x hybridus* H
Lungwort *Pulmonaria saccharata* H
Marsh marigold *Caltha palustris* H
Narrow-leaved lungwort *Pulmonaria angustifolia* H
Primrose *Primula vulgaris* H
Spurge *Euphorbia* H S
Star of Bethlehem *Ornithogalum umbellatum* B
Wallflower *Erysimum cheiri* Bi

Summer

June–August
Annual mallow *Malope trifida* A
Bay tree *Laurus nobilis* S
Beauty berry *Callicarpa bodinieri var. giraldii* S
Bee-bee tree *Tetradium daniellii* T
Bell heather *Erica cinerea* S
Bergamot *Monarda didyma* H
Bistort *Polygonum bistorta* H
Blanket flower *Gaillardia grandiflora* H
Blue lace flower *Trachymene coerulea* A
Borage *Borago officinalis* A
Boston ivy *Parthenocissus tricuspidata* C
Buddleia *Buddleia davidii* S

Burning bush *Dictamnus albus* H
California bluebell *Phacelia campanularia* A
Californian poppy *Eschscholzia californica* A
Canterbury bells *Campanula medium* B
Caryopteris *Caryopteris clandonensis* S
Catmint *Nepeta* H
Chamomile, dog fennel *Anthemis tinctoria* H
China aster, open-centred *Callistephus chinensis* A
Chives *Allium schoenoprasum* B
Climbing hydrangea *Hydrangea anomala* subsp. *petiolaris* H
Climbing hydrangea *Pileostegia viburnoides* C
Columbine *Aquilegia* spp. H
Common honeysuckle, woodbine *Lonicera periclymenum* C
Common jasmine *Jasminum officinale* C
Common mullein *Verbascum thapsiforme* Bi
Coneflower *Echinacea purpurea* H
Creeping zinnia *Sanvitalia procumbens* A
Crested poppy *Argemone platyceras* A or H
Culver's root *Veronicastrum virginicum* H
Cupid's dart *Catananche caerulea* H
Dahlia 'Amazone' or 'Moonfire', open-centred flower type *Dahlia* H
Daisy bush *Olearia x haastii* S
Delphinium, semi-double flowers *Delphinium elatum* H
Delphinium, single-flowered cultivars *Delphinium* H
Dog rose *Rosa canina* S
English lavender *Lavandula angustifolia* S
Escallonia *Escallonia langleyensis* S
Evening primrose *Oenothera biennis* Bi
Fennel *Foeniculum vulgare* H
Floss flower *Ageratum houstonianum* A
Forget-me-not *Myosotis* spp. B
Foxglove *Digitalis purpurea* Bi

French lavender *Lavandula stoechas* S
French marigold *Tagetes patula* A
Fuchsia, hardy *Fuchsia* cultivars eg. *magellanica* S
Garden mint *Mentha spicata* H
Giant angelica *Angelica gigas* Bi
Giant bellflower *Campanula latifolia* H
Giant fennel *Ferula communis* H
Giant knapweed *Centaurea macrocephala* H
Golden rain tree *Koelreuteria paniculata* T
Golden rod *Solidago* spp. & cultivars H
Guelder rose *Viburnum opulus* S
Hawthorn *Crataegus monogyna* S or T
Hedgehog rose, Japanese rose *Rosa rugosa* S
Herringbone cotoneaster *Cotoneaster horizontalis* S
Holly *Ilex aquifolium* T
Hollyhock, single-flowered *Alcea rosea* Bi
Hoptree *Ptelea trifoliata* S
Hyssop *Hyssopus officinalis* S
Ice plant *Sedum spectabile* H
Indian bean tree *Catalpa bignonioides* T
Jacob's ladder *Polemonium caeruleum* H
Joe-pye weed *Eupatorium purpureum* H
Ling, Scotch heather *Calluna vulgaris* S
Love-in-a-mist *Nigella damascena* A
Macedonian scabious *Knautia macedonica* H
Mallow *Lavatera trimestris* A
Marigold, single-flowered *Calendula officinalis* A
Masterwort *Astrantia major* H
Moroccan toadflax *Linaria maroccana* A
Nasturtium *Tropaeolum majus* A
Oleaster *Elaeagnus angustifolia* S
Orange ball tree *Buddleia globosa* S

Oriental poppy *Papaver orientale* H

Ox-eye daisy *Leucanthemum vulgare* H

Peony, single-flowered cultivars *paeonia* H

Perennial phlox *Phlox paniculata* H

Perennial sweet pea *Lathyrus latifolius* H

Perennial wallflower *Cheiranthus 'Bowles's Mauve'* S

Poached-egg plant *Limnanthes douglasii* A

Potentilla *Potentilla nepalensis 'Miss Willmott'* H

Purple loosestrife *Lythrum salicaria* H

Purple toadflax *Linaria purpurea* H

Queen Anne's thimbles *Gilia capitata* A

Red valerian *Centranthus ruber* H

Rosemary *Rosmarinus officinalis* S

Runner bean *Phaseolus coccineus* A

Scabious *Scabiosa caucasica* H

Sea lavender *Limonium latifolium* H

Shrubby hare's ear *Bupleurum fruticosum* S

Siberian wallflower *Erysimum hieraciifolium* H

Small-leaved cotoneaster *Cotoneaster microphyllus* S

Snapdragon *Antirrhinum majus* A or H

Sneezeweed *Helenium 'Moerheim Beauty'* H

Snowberry *Symphoricarpos albus* S

Sunflower, avoid pollen-free cultivars *Helianthus annuus* A

Sweet alyssum *Lobularia maritima* A

Sweet briar, eglantine *Rosa eglanteria* S

Sweet rocket/dame's violet *Hesperis matronalis* H

Sweet scabious *Scabiosa atropurpurea* A

Sweet william *Dianthus barbatus* Bi

Tamarisk *Tamarix ramosissima* S

Teasel *Dipsacus fullonum* Bi

Thrift *Armeria maritima* H

Thyme *Thymus* spp. & cultivars S

Tobacco *Nicotiana alata* A
Trailing bellflower *Campanula poscharskyana* H
Tree mallow *Lavatera olbia* S
Trumpet vine *Campsis radicans* C
Verbena *Verbena bonariensis* H & *Verbena rigida* A
Veronica *Veronica longifolia* H
Viper's bugloss *Echium vulgare* A
Virginia creeper *Parthenocissus quinquefolia* C
Weigela *Weigela florida* S
Wild angelica *Angelica sylvestris* Bi
Wild marjoram *Origanum vulgare* H
Yellow cosmos *Cosmos sulphureus* A
Yellow ox-eye daisy *Buphthalmum salicifolium* H

Autumn

September–October
Autumn crocus *Colchicum* spp. B
Autumn ox-eye *Leucanthemella serotina* H
Aster *Aster amellus, A. lateriflorus var horizontalis, A. thomsoni 'nanus'* H
Blue-flowered leadwort *Ceratostigma plumbaginoides* H
Chrysanthemum, open-centred flower forms *Chrysanthemum* H
Clematis *Clematis heracleifolia* C
Common ivy *Hedera* C
Crocus *Crocus speciosus* B
Dahlia *Dahlia elaeagnus pungens* S
Holly *Ilex aquifolium* T
Japanese aralia *Fatsia japonica* S
Mexican bush sage *Salvia leucantha* H
Michaelmas daisy *Aster amellus, A. lateriflorus var horizontalis, A. novae-angliae, A. novi-belgii, A. thomsoni 'nanus'* H
Persian ivy *Hedera colchica* C
Strawberry tree *Arbutus unedo* S or T

Sunflower *Helianthus x laetiflorus* H

Tansy-leaved Aster, Tahoka daisy *Machaeranthera tanacetifolia* A

Winter

November–February

Christmas rose *Helleborus niger* H

Clematis *Clematis cirrhosa* C

Crocus *Crocus biflorus* & *Crocus tommasinianus* B

Honeysuckle *Lonicera x purpusii* S

Laurustinus *Viburnum tinus* S

Oregon grape *Mahonia x media* S

Snowdrop *Galanthus nivalis* B

Stinking hellebore *Helleborus foetidus* H

Winter aconite *Eranthis hyemalis* B

Winter Box *Sarcococca Hookeriana* S

A BUTTERFLY BORDER

Butterflies, together with moths, are insects that form the order known as Lepidoptera. They both have caterpillars – larvae that feed on the foliage and flowers of their host plants. They then crawl away to sheltered places where they pupate and later emerge as adult butterflies.

There are fifty-nine butterfly species resident in Britain, plus up to thirty others that come here as migrants from mainland Europe. Some butterfly species require specialised habitats, such as broadleaved woodland or heaths and so are unlikely to be seen in the back garden. Twelve or so species, however, are amenable to wooing. All you have to do is:

- Stop using pesticides.
- Provide warmth and shelter. Butterflies like to bask in sunshine, which raises their body temperature so they are able

to fly and remain active. A few flat stones in a non-windy, open place make ideal 'warming pads'.

- Provide plants for caterpillars (see below).
- Grow a range of colourful flowers to provide nectar for the flying season, March to October.

TOP TEN FLOWERS FOR BUTTERFLIES

Generally, the same nectar-rich flowers that are good for bees are good for butterflies. The sweet fluid is the plant's reward to the butterfly (or bee) for pollination. But individual butterfly species do have preferences, and the following list will also ensure nectar from March to October. As a rule British butterflies prefer purple, pink and yellow coloured blossoms; and, like bees, butterflies find tubular or flat-topped single flowers easiest to extract nectar from.

Where possible plant in clumps. Not only does it look good, it does the butterflies good by making the plants easy to find. That said, even if you only have space for one of these plants you will be helping to conserve these national natural treasures. Almost three-quarters of UK butterfly species have decreased in population during the last decade. In return, your garden will be enriched by the bright colours of these captivating insects. They are a true garden display.

Buddleia *Buddleia davidii*
Also known as the butterfly bush. Attracts red admiral, small tortoiseshell, comma, peacock, large white, small white, brimstone, meadow brown.

Verbena esp. *Verbena bonariensis*
Red admiral, large white, comma.

Sweet rocket *Hesperis matronalis*
Flowers in spring/early summer. Attractive to small white and orange-tip. Violet-like in its fragrance.

Ivy *Hedera helix*
The evergreen climbing vine provides winter nectar. Useful for red admiral, comma.

Honesty *Lunaria annua*
Tall plant with heart-shaped leaves and sweet-smelling pink or violet-purple flowers from April to June.

Hemp agrimony *Eupatorium cannabinum* or **Joe-pye weed** *Eupatorium purpureum*
Red admiral, comma, speckled wood.

Red valerian *Centranthus ruber*
A cottage garden plant that produces clusters of red flowers from mid-summer through to autumn. Great for dry soil.

Michaelmas daisy *Aster* **spp**.
Red admiral.

Lavender *Lavandula* **spp.**
Large white, small white, gatekeeper.

Field scabious *Knautia arvensis*
Meadow brown, gatekeeper, small tortoiseshell, painted lady.

Other floral butterfly-attractors

Herbaceous perennials
Alyssum (*Aurinia saxatilis*), aubrieta (*Aubrieta deltoidea*), bugbane (*Actaea simplex*), bugle (*Ajuga reptans*), catmint (*Nepeta X faassenii*), *Centaurea* spp. (e.g. *C. dealbata*, *C. Montana*), Dahlia – single-flowered varieties, spear mint (*Mentha spicata*), globe artichoke (*Cynara scolymus*), globe thistles (*Echinops* spp.), golden rod (*Solidago* spp.), hyssop (*Hyssopus officinalis*), ice plant (*Sedum spectabile*), Jacob's ladder (*Polemonium caeruleum*), perennial candytuft (*Iberis sempervirens*), phlox (*Phlox paniculata*), scabious

(*Scabiosa* spp.), soapwort (*Saponaria* spp., especially *S. ocymoides*), thrift (*Armeria* spp.), water mint (*Mentha aquatica*).

Annual and biennials

African marigold (*Tagetes erecta*), alyssum (*Lobularia maritima*), candytuft (*Iberis amara*), China aster (*Callistephus chinensis*), cornflower (*Centaurea cyanus*), French marigold (*Tagetes patula*), heliotrope/cherry pie (*Heliotropium* cultivars), marigold (*Calendula officinalis*), mignonette (*Reseda odorata*), stocks (*Matthiola incana* & hybrids), sweet william (*Dianthus barbatus*), verbena (*Verbena rigida*), wallflower (*Erysimum cheiri*), zinnia (*Zinnia elegans*).

Shrubs

Blackberry (*Rubus fruticosus*), hawthorn (*Crataegus monogyna*), heather (*Calluna vulgaris*), heath (*Erica* spp.), daboecia (*Daboecia cantabrica*), hebe spp., Japanese spiraea (*Spiraea japonica*), marjoram (*Origanum vulgare*), Oregon grape (*Mahonia aquifolium*), willow (*Salix* spp., especially male forms of *Salix caprea*), thyme (*Thymus* spp.).

WILDLIFE TO WATCH OUT FOR

The twelve butterflies species most likely to visit your garden are peacock, red admiral, small cabbage white, large cabbage white, brimstone, painted lady, comma, green-veined white, orange-tip, speckled wood, meadow brown, small copper.

Tip: Leave fallen fruit. In late summer/early autumn some butterflies will feast on the juice of the windfalls. Anything rotten in the fruit bowl can also be put out for them.

TOP TEN HOST FLOWERS AND PLANTS FOR CATERPILLARS

Unlike an adult butterfly, the larval stage is fussy and atavistic in its eating habits. Caterpillars almost exclusively chew on wild native plants. Weeds, in other words. You can now pass off the overgrown corner you have not got around to weeding and the unmown lawn as your caterpillar garden.

Thistles *Cirsium* spp. & *Carduus* spp.
For the larval stages of the painted lady and American painted lady.

Lady's smock *Cardamine partensis*
Orange-tip and green-veined white.

Meadow grasses – eg fescues (*Festuca* spp.), bentgrass (*Agrostis* spp.), Yorkshire fog (*Holcus lanatus*), false broom (*Brachypodium sylvaticum*), timothy (*Phleum pratense*), cocksfoot (*Dactylis glomerata*).
   Meadow brown, speckled wood, wall butterfly, gatekeeper, marbled white, ringlet, small heath, Essex skipper, large skipper and small skipper. The requirements of grassland butterflies vary somewhat – as to which grasses they prefer, and whether the sward is dry or damp – but if you don't cut between March and August, and not below 5cm, you will not go far wrong. A wildflower lawn is a haven for Lepidoptera.

Bird's-foot trefoil *Lotus corniculatus*
Common blue, dingy skipper, green hairstreak, short-tailed blue, wood white, silver-studded blue, clouded yellow.

Stinging nettle *Urtica dioica*
Red admiral, peacock, comma and small tortoiseshell. Cut the patch back by about half in June to provide new shoots for the mid-summer broods of caterpillars.

Holly *Ilex*
Holly blue.

Red clover *Trifolium pratense*
Mazarine blue, short-tailed blue.

Broad-leaved dock *Rumex obtusifolius*
Small copper.

Blackberry *Rubus fruticosus*
Holly blue, green hairstreak, grizzled skipper.

Blackthorn *Prunus spinosa*
Black hairstreak, black-veined white, brown hairstreak, scarce swallowtail.

As every gardener knows, there are two butterflies whose offspring do not share the general predilection of caterpillars to munch native weeds. These are the large cabbage white and the small cabbage white who like to gnaw brassicas and nasturtiums (*Tropaeolum*) above all else. So when the wildlife gets too much, try these measures: fine mesh netting will prevent the butterflies from reaching the brassicas and nasturtiums to lay eggs; otherwise the eggs, when laid, can be rubbed off. Usually the eggs are laid on the underside of the leaves. Caterpillars themselves can also be picked off. You might try a soapy water spray. Use a natural, vegetable soap. The surfactants in the soap cover the breathing holes of the caterpillars so that they suffocate.

Tip: As well as providing food for the caterpillars of holly blue, green hairstreak and grizzled skipper, the bramble provides nectar for adults of other butterfly species. To economise on space in the garden, grow the bramble over your log pile. You also get the benefit of picking blackberries, the bramble's fruits.

MOTHS

Few people find moths as enchanting as their daytime relatives. Their cause is not helped by the habit of some moths of eating clothes. Or, indeed, the profusion of moth species – over 2,500 in the UK – which can make identifying individual species irritatingly tricky.

Love or loathe moths, they are a vital part of the night-time food chain for bats, spiders, owls and mammals. Daytime predators, especially small perching birds, eat sleeping moths if they uncover them along with their caterpillar offspring. Many moths are also excellent plant pollinators. They deserve – and need – a place in the garden.

To invite moths into your garden, plant night-flowering, nectar-rich plants, many of which have specifically evolved to attract nocturnal insects. Most moth flowers are white or pale coloured, so that moths can see them at dusk. An 'ordinary' urban garden attracts around 100 moth species over the year. A moth-friendly garden should easily attract 250 moth species a year.

A moth garden will also be a fragrant retreat for you.

Not all moths are creatures of the night. One day-time moth to look out for is the hummingbird hawkmoth, which hovers in front of flowers as it sucks out nectar through its long thin tongue. It is a migrant to southern Britain in warm summers.

TOP TEN PLANTS FOR MOTHS

Evening primrose *Oenothera* spp.
Flowers remain closed during the day, then uncurl at dusk.

Tobacco plant *Nicotiana affinis*
This flowering tobacco plant is sweetly scented and a magnet for

moths. The luminous white salver-shaped flowers grow up to 9cm long in the summer. Prefers fertile, moist but well-drained soil in sun or partial shade. A biennial, easily grown from seed.

Night-scented stock *Matthiola bicornis*
A magnet for moths. Not good on acid soils.

Buddleia 'White Profusion' *Buddleia davidii*
Luminous, white variety of buddleia with fragrant flowers. Hugely attractive to moths.

Bluebeard *Caryopteris x clandonensi*
A shrub whose blue flowers glow in moonlight.

Giant sea holly 'Silver Ghost' *Eryngium giganteum*
A showy plant, which grows up to 90cm, and produces silvery-white metallic heads in its second year.

Hebe 'Great Orme' *Plantaginaceae*
Produces spikes of pink-white flowers in summer/autumn.

Honeysuckle *Lonicera* spp.
There are about 180 species of honeysuckle, all magnets for moths. The *L. Caprifolium* is guaranteed to bloom early – mid May is the usual date. The flowers are creamy white when they first open and deepen to pink as they age. It climbs to 3m. Unfussy and easy to grow.

Jasmine *Jasminum officinale*
A white-flowering jasmine.

Bell heather *Erica cinerea*
Produces honey scent from pink flowers.

Also consider: Night-flowering catchfly (*Silene noctiflora*), pinks (*Dianthus* spp. esp *D. plumarius*), bladder campion (*Silene vulgaris*), sweet william (*Dianthus barbatus*) – but only the single-flowered, old fashioned, cottage-garden kind.

To provide for the caterpillars of moths, leave knapweeds (*Centaurea*), long grass and thistles (*Asteraceae*) in wilder corners of the garden. Lady's bedstraw (*Galium verum*) is food for the extraordinary elephant hawkmoth caterpillar. Native trees and hedging plants, such as birch (*Betula*), oak (*Quercus robur*), willow (*salix*) and hawthorn (*Crataegus monogyna*), host many moth caterpillars.

Tip: To discover the multitude of moth species in your garden, make a moth 'trap'. Simply suspend a bright white light (such as an inspection lamp, with suitable RCD circuit breaker) over a white cotton sheet, and the moths will land on the sheet. Have handy a good identification guide, such as Paul Waring and Martin Parson's *Field Guide to the Moths of Great Britain and Ireland*.

A BIRD BORDER

Imagine a garden without birds. Birds are the soul of the garden. Their song uplifts, their behaviour fascinates and their beauty cheers up grey days. A well-stocked bird border will help our feathered friends through difficult days – which, with demanding, hungry fledglings to feed can come in summer as well as winter – and attract new visitors too.

A bird border should also offer shelter. Since birds can be sensitive to human noise and disturbance, the border should be situated in a quiet area of the garden, ideally with a creeper-covered fence or hedge as the boundary, which can be used as a nesting site and a roost, as well as a restaurant. Bare fences are anathema to birds. Plant cover in the form of shrubs, trees and climbers is vital. Think mixed hedges of hawthorn (*Crataegus monogyna*), holly

(*Ilex*), dog rose (*Rosa canina*), goat willow (*Salix caprea*), honeysuckle (*Lonicera periclymenum*) and ivy (*Hedera*). The bird border does not have to be a wilderness. On the contrary, the idea – as with bee and butterfly borders – is to make a flora feature that is attractive to man and beast.

Unlike bees and butterflies, bird species have a diverse range of eating requirements. Some are vegetarian seed eaters, others are keen carnivores. Try to bear this in mind when planning the bird border. Otherwise, there are few rules to follow. The border needs to provide food through all the seasons, and it makes aesthetic sense for humans and practical sense for birds if the border has trees at the back, shrubs in the middle and smaller herbaceous plants at the front.

Large forest trees such as the mighty oak are impractical in most gardens. But there are smaller deciduous trees which will fit town gardens and give big benefit to wildlife, among them holly (*Ilex aquifolium*), crab apple (*Malus* spp.), rowan (*Sorbus aucuparia*) and cornelian cherry (*Cornus mas*). All four provide fruit, somewhere to nest and a look-out station. Birds often like to check out the lie of the land before landing to feed to ensure there are no predators lurking. A tree is also somewhere for a bird to sing from. In a larger garden, you could consider a larch (*Larix*), willow (*Salix*) or ash (*Fraxinus*).

Consider woody shrubs which provide cover and protection in winter as well as summer. The semi-evergreen barberry (*Berberis thunbergii atropurpurea*) looks good, has thorns to deter any cat, and it produces a rich crop of autumn berries. Other spiky providers of autumn berries are the evergreen Oregon grape (*Mahonia aquifolium*) and firethorn (*Pyracantha coccinea*).

At the front of the border, there should be a range of annual and herbaceous plants which produce nectar to attract insects and ideally set with seed for songbirds in late summer. Do ignore advice which instructs you to use native species only. After all, many old-fashioned cottage garden flowers are not native, yet make a feast for birds' beaks and human eyes.

TOP TEN PLANTS FOR A BIRD BORDER

Hawthorn *Crataegus*

No less than 365 insect species have been recorded on the hawthorn, which can be grown as a tree, large shrub or hedge. Its prickly nature offers first-class protection, and its berries or 'haws' are scoffed by birds in autumn. If grown as a shrub it requires cutting down to the base every decade or so.

Also consider two other natives: hazel (*Corylus avellana*), which can be grown as a multi-stemmed shrub up to 5m in height, and the nuts of which attract jays, woodpigeons, nuthatches and woodpeckers. Meanwhile, the fast growing silver birch (*Betula pendula*) supports more than 300 different insect species, and its white peeling bark and delicate, ethereal branches bring interest to a winter garden.

Crab apple (*Malus sylvestris*)

An attractive native tree which grows up to 10m tall in the wild, but is available in smaller cultivated forms from suppliers. Produces an abundance of blossom in spring, and much sought-after fruit in autumn. The tree supports over 100 insect species. *Malus* 'John Downie' is a small, vigorous variety with eye-catching red-green apples.

Also consider: rowan or mountain ash (*Sorbus aucuparia*) which is a notably compact, decorative tree that is usefully tolerant of pollution and famous for the bright red berries that follow on from its springtime white flowers. The attractive cornelian cherry (*Cornus mas*) produces fruit in summer, when there can be a surprising gap in natural food for birds. The pale flowers perfectly offset the dark green of holly at the back of a border. Spindleberry (*Euonymus europaeus*) is a safe choice for alkaline soil. Despite its exotic pink fruits it is a native shrub.

Teasel *Dipsacus fullonum*

The seed heads are a magnet for goldfinches and crossbills. The plant's striking architecture is a bonus in the winter garden. Easy to grow. Indeed, its habit of self-seeding will require weeding to keep it under control.

Sunflower *Helianthus annuus*

The large striped 'seeds' that pack the sunflower head are actually a type of dry fruit called achene. Technicalities aside, many birds flock to eat the oil-rich hearts of the achene, including siskins, chaffinches, house sparrows, long-tailed tits and greenfinches. Plant at the back of the border; the sunflower can reach 3m in height.

Cotoneaster *Cotoneaster* spp.

With more than 200 different species, cotoneaster comes in numerous shapes and sizes. There is almost certainly one to suit your border. What cotoneasters have in common is nectar-rich small whiteish-pink flowers and a crop of nutritious berries, generally red but sometimes yellow, on which starlings and the thrush family gorge. Waxwings love it too. Two worth trying are *C. horizontalis*, a spreading deciduous variety, and *C. lacteus*, an upright ornamental evergreen shrub which can reach 4m in height. The latter's foliage provides colour in winter, as well as roosts for small perching birds. Maintenance of any cotoneaster is minimal.

Guelder rose *Viburnum opulus*

A native deciduous shrub which bears clumps of succulent glossy berries through the winter. Can also be incorporated into a hedge.

Golden rod *Solidago virgaurea*

Traditional border plant, which produces spikes of deep yellow nectar-laden flowers over summer and autumn. Produces seeds beloved of linnets and is a popular over-wintering hotel for insects. Thrives on poor soil.

Barberry *Berberis darwinii*
A native of South America, this particular member of the vast Berberis family is an evergreen shrub which produces rich orange flowers. These are followed by bird-friendly blue-black round fruits (which are mildly toxic to humans). Looks striking almost all the year round and grows 1.5–2m in height. Wrens and other small perching birds sometimes nest amid its spine-toothed leaves. *B. thunbergii* and *B. aggregata* provide berries into autumn and winter.

Love-Lies-Bleeding *Amaranthus caudatus*
This annual has everything, from striking looks (spectacular cascades of deep red tassels) to a scent that attracts butterflies and other insects, plus seed heads that will sate the appetite of the hungriest finch.

Anise Hyssop *Agastache foeniculum*
A perennial that bears lilac (sometimes white) flowers on spikes about 60cm high. These attract insects from far and wide. Seed-eating birds will gorge on the seeds in winter.

Tip: Plant lavender to attract blue tits to the garden. Blue tits use it in their nests as an anti-bacterial agent. The seeds are also prized by a whole range of birds.

PLANTS FOR BIRDS BY FOOD TYPE

If you wish to plan a flower or herbaceous border principally for its usefulness as a food source for birds here is a quick guide.

Berry-producing plants for birds
Barberry *Berberis darwinii*/*B. thunbergii*, *B. aggregata*
Bird cherry *Prunus padus*

Blackberry *Rubus fruticosus* agg.

Blackcurrant *Ribes nigrum*

Blackthorn *Prunus spinosa*

Cornelian cherry *Cornus mas*

Cotoneaster spp. (especially *C. bullatus*, *C. cornubia* hybrids, *C. horizontalis*, *C. Lacteus*)

Crab apple *Malus sylvestris*

Dog rose *Rosa canina*

Dogwood *Cornus alba*/*Cornus stolonifera*

Elder *Sambucus nigra*

Firethorn *Pyracantha*

Gean/wild cherry *Prunus avium*

Guelder rose *Viburnum opulus*

Hawthorn *Crataegus monogyna*/Midlands hawthorn *Crataegus laevigata*

Holly *Ilex aquifolium*

Honeysuckle *Lonicera periclymenun*/Perfoliate honeysuckle *Lonicera caprifolium*

Ivy *Hedera helix*

Mezereon *Daphne mezereon*

Mistletoe *Viscum album*

Oregon grape *Mahonia aquifolium*

Photinia *Photinia davidiana*

Rowan *Sorbus aucuparia*

Sea-buckthorn *Hippophae rhamnoides*

Spindleberry *Euonymus europaeus*

Wayfaring tree *Viburnum lantana*

Whitebeam *Sorbus aria*

Wild privet *Ligustrum vulgare*

Wild service tree *Sorbus torminalis*

Yew *Taxus baccata*

Seed-producing plants for birds

Alder *Alnus glutinosa*

Beech *Fagus sylvatica*

Dandelion *Taraxacum* agg.

Devil's bit scabious *Succisa pratensis*

Evening primrose *Oenothera biennis*

Field scabious *Knautia arvensis*

Golden rod *Solidago virgaurea*

Greater knapweed *Centaurea scabiosa*

Hazel *Corylus avellana*

Honesty *Lunaria annua*

Hornbeam *Carpinus betulus*

Lavender *Lavandula*

Lemon balm *Melissa officinalis*

Silver birch *Betula pendula*

Sunflower *Helianthus annuus*

Teasel *Dipsacus fullonum*

Thistles *Carduus/Cirsium*

Plants to avoid bringing into the garden

These are invasive species, domestic and foreign:

Canadian golden rod *Solidago canadensis, S. altissima*

Giant hogweed *Heracleum mantegazzianum*

Giant rhubarb *Gunnera* spp.

Himalayan balsam, Indian balsam *Impatiens glandulifera*

Hottentot fig *Carpobrotus edulis*

Japanese knotweed *Fallopia japonica*

Japanese rose *Rosa rugosa*

Montbretia *Crocosmia x crocosmiiflora*

Russian vine *Fallopia baldschuanica*

Spanish bluebells *Hyacinthoides hispanica*

Variegated yellow archangel *Lamium galeobdolon*

Three-cornered garlic *Allium triquetrum*

BIRDS TO WATCH OUT FOR

Wren

The tiny wren will flit in and out the foliage looking for food. According to myth, it is the King of Birds, after it bested the eagle in a competition to see who could fly the highest. The eagle soared as high as it could go, not realising that the wren was hiding on its back. When the eagle reached the apex of its flight, the wren fluttered up to win by a few inches. A diminutive bird with a voice as massive as its cunning. The males make a selection of nests, of which a female chooses one. Hopefully.

Blackcap

A greyish sparrow-sized warbler, with a delightful fluting song. The male has a black cap, the female a chestnut one. Primarily a summer visitor, although birds from north-east Europe are increasingly spending the winter in the UK.

Robin

The pin-up bird of the Christmas card industry. This little thrush is one of the principal habitués of the border, where it pokes about for tiny insects and seeds. They can become very tame, and are quite likely to hop about next to you while you dig, or even eat from your hand. They suffer slightly from the Napoleon complex, being tiny but aggressive to other robins who stray on their patch. Males and females look identical.

Blackbird

Confusingly, only the male is black; the female is dark chocolate brown. A fixture of flower borders and lawns, they are one of the commonest UK species, with some 5 million pairs breeding here. (The population in winter goes up to 10 million and more.) Like other members of the thrush family, they are superb singers, and the blackbird's melancholic evensong is the soundtrack which plays out the day in many a garden.

Jay
Properly a woodland bird, the raucous, pink-hued jay often visits flower borders in autumn to bury acorns and hazelnuts as a food store. A single jay can bury up to 3,000 acorns in a month, making them important natural planters of oaks. A member of the crow family, the jay is also a mimic to rival a myna bird.

Fieldfares
Migrant members of the thrush family, fieldfares are really birds of open countryside. However, they will flock to gardens to feed on berries and fruits in harsh weather. In former times it was prized as a game bird, but it is currently on the European Red List.

PROJECTS FOR SMALL SPACES: TUBS, CONTAINERS AND HANGING BASKETS

Containers are a cunning way of attracting wildlife to areas where you can't plant directly into the ground or to the more formal parts of your garden. For smaller gardens, patios and balconies, containers are perfect.

Garden centres and shops have an array of containers, troughs and tubs for every budget and taste. Old chimney pots make excellent plant containers, as do old metal buckets, soup tureens, cauldrons, sinks and tin baths.

Planting herbs and nectar-rich plants will attract important pollinators like bees, butterflies and ladybirds, which in turn will attract birds and small mammals. With a little ingenuity you can have a whole mini-habitat in a container – a butterfly border in a basket, a moth haven in a pot – or you can simply plant some herbs in a box outside the kitchen window, where they are easy to access for cooking and where bees will enjoy their flowers. Marjoram, rosemary, sage and thyme are as popular with bees as they are with cooks. Climbers are easily grown in containers against a trellis and can hide unsightly walls; the same climbers will make a 'living wall' which will provide food and shelter for birds and insects.

Almost as easy as a herb pot is a wildflower meadow in a tub. Buy a packet of mixed native wildflower seeds, sprinkle onto peat-free compost in the spring, keep watering, and watch ox-eye daisies, cornflowers, campions and harebells come up.

Tip: Nobody ever went wrong by planting a container full of nasturtiums. Their flowers make an indulgence for the eyes, and their nectar a banquet for butterflies and bees. They can be trailed up, trailed down and trailed along. Cabbage white caterpillars eat the leaves, or you can put the leaves and flowers in a salad for yourself.

STEP-BY-STEP: MAKE A NECTAR-RICH FLOWER GARDEN IN A POT

You can create a wildlife haven on the smallest balcony, and it doesn't have to be a thicket of weeds. A single, large container will do if it contains plants with nectar and pollen to attract and feed butterflies, bees, hoverflies and other insects. The display can provide shelter for insects to roost or hibernate and food plants for various caterpillars.

Step 1. Put a large pot or planter in its final position. (Remember to use lightweight containers on balconies.)

Step 2. Fill the bottom of the pot with inverted yogurt pots, broken polystyrene or cracked china for drainage.

Step 3. Half fill with peat-free compost.

Step 4. Plant with small-growing varieties of lavender (*Lavandula*), catmint (*Nepeta*), *Geranium*, *Salvia*, *Sedum spectabile*, *Achillea* and *Phlox*. The taller flowers should be at the back, the lowest growing at the front. A few bulbs of spring flowers – snowdrops (*Galanthus* *nivalis*), *Narcissus* and aconites (*Eranthis hyemalis*) – will provide welcome early nectar and colour.

Step 5. Top up with compost, until 5cm from top.

Step 6. Water well (at least once a day in summer).

Step 7. Add a bee hotel. Pack a short length of terracotta pipe with hollow stems, such as bamboo or hogweed, with ends facing out.

PLANTS FOR CONTAINERS

With all the plants suggested choose smaller growing varieties – then they won't need unsightly staking or be out of proportion with your container. The choice is vast, but always try to choose single-flowered varieties because they have accessible nectar for bees and butterflies.

A miniature cornfield meadow

Poppy (*Papaver rhoeas*), corn cockle (*Agrostemma githago*), pheasant's eye (*Adonis annua*), wild pansy (*Viola tricolor*), cornflower (*Centaurea cyanus*).

A miniature woodland glade

For shady, shadowed areas: Primrose (*Primula vulgaris*), ivy (*Hedera*), wood avens (*Geum urbanum*), bugle (*Ajuga*), bluebell (*Hyacinthoides non-scripta*), red campion (*Silene dioica*), foxglove (*Digitalis*), wood forget-me-not (*Myosotis sylvatica*).

A miniature wildflower meadow

Creeping thyme (*Thymus serpyllum*), harebell (*Campanula rotundifolia*), meadow clary (*Salvia pratensis*), cowslip (*Primula veris*), sheep's bit scabious (*Jasione montana*), ox-eye daisy (*Leucanthemum vulgare*), kidney vetch (*Anthyllis vulneraria*).

Trees

If you have room, trees and large shrubs make surprisingly good container plants. Drought-tolerant species are best. A bay tree

(*Laurus nobilis*) always impresses (and you can use the leaves), while buddleia is guaranteed to bring butterflies, bees and moths flocking – there are numerous dwarf varieties. Mexican orange blossom (*Choisya ternate*) is an attractive shrub which produces masses of sweetly fragranced white flowers in summer.

Climbers
Broad-leaved everlasting pea, clematis (especially *Clematis x cartmanii*, an evergreen with springtime white blooms), ivy (try *Hedera helix* 'Ivalace', which has curled edges), honeysuckle (*Lonicera periclymenum*).

Herbs
Winter savoury (*Satureja montana*), borage (*Borago officinalis*), chives (*Allium schoenoprasum*), hyssop (*Hyssopus officinalis*), lavender (*Lavandula*), lemon balm (*Melissa officinalis*), golden marjoram (*Origanum vulgare* 'Aureum'), thyme (*Thymus vulgaris*), mint (*Mentha sachalinensis*), sage (*Salvia officinalis*). Cut back in spring to keep the plants healthy.

Tip: Don't forget to add a bird bath or drinker to your container collection. A weighted-down large saucer full of water will slake the thirst of small birds all the year round.

MAINTENANCE

Undoubtedly the one drawback with containers is watering. During the summer you will need to water every day, at least. You may want to install an irrigation system if manual watering with a can is difficult or a chore to do. Grouping containers together will reduce the workload of watering. Grouped pots also create a humid micro-climate that attracts wildlife. Line unglazed pots with polythene to reduce water loss. Slim-line water butts allow you to collect rainwater while taking up a minimum of space.

STEP-BY-STEP: MAKE A WILDFLOWER HANGING BASKET

Hanging baskets are another good way of introducing plants for wildlife into small spaces.

Step 1. Rest the basket on an open bucket or china mixing bowl for stability. Line it with a woolly jumper cut to size. Alternatively, use a synthetic liner – but never sphagnum moss gathered from the wild as this is unsustainable. You may wish to incorporate water-absorbing gel to reduce watering.

Step 2. Using sharp scissors make a series of 5cm slits in the sides of the basket liner to accommodate trailing plants. (If the basket is large and deep enough, two layers of slits can be made around the basket.)

Step 3. Fill with peat-free compost up to the first layer of slits.

Step 4. Insert the trailing plants (see below) by pushing the plants 'head-first' from the inside through the slits. You may find this easier if you wrap a tube of plastic or polythene around the heads, and unwrap it when finished.

Step 5. Tease out roots of the trailing plants, and add more compost.

Step 6. Plant the tallest plant in your selection in the centre.

Step 7. Add a little more compost, then plant the 'mid height' ones around it.

Step 8. Add more compost, and plant the smallest plants around the edge. You should finish with a layer of compost and plants 3cm below the edge.

Step 9. Water well, and frequently in summer.

WILDLIFE-FRIENDLY PLANTS FOR HANGING BASKETS

Centre basket
Lavender (*Lavendula*), scabious (*Scabiosa*), snapdragon (*Antirrhinum*), ox-eye daisy (*Leucanthemum vulgare*), catmint (especially *Nepeta x faassenii*), sorrel (*Rumex acetosa*).

Mid-basket to edge
Verbena x hybrida, white alyssum (*Lobularia maritime*), Petunias, chives (*Allium schoenoprasum*), thyme (*Thymus vulgaris*), creeping thyme (*Thymus serpyllum*), dwarf lavender, wild pansy (*Viola tricolor*), Aubretia, parsley (*Petroselinum crispum*), dwarf hebes (try *H. pinguifolia* 'Pagei'), strawberries (*Fragaria x ananassa*).

Trailing
Nasturtium (*Tropaeolum*), sweet pea (*Lathyrus odoratus*), *Lobelia* 'Pendula', ivy (*Hedera*), ivy-leaved pelargoniums (*Pelargonium peltatum*), trailing fuchsias, poached-egg plant (*Limnanthes douglasii*), bird's-foot trefoil (*Lotus corniculatus*), trailing verbena (try *V.* 'Homestead Purple').

CHAPTER 5
TREES AND WOODLAND GLADES

Many of our commonest garden inhabitants originally lived in woodlands, which have suffered enormous declines in extent across the UK. While deep woodland can never be replicated exactly in a garden, in fact most wildlife activity occurs in the margins or in the glades of woods where there is more light. By artful planning, you can compress what in a real forest or wood might require an acre into a miniature-reserve in the corner of the garden. Trees do not have to be large to be effective for wildlife. Certainly the mighty oak hosts more species than any other native tree, but the hawthorn and the silver birch are not far behind. Both are suitable for small and medium gardens.

From the point of view of a bird, a bat, a butterfly or other flying insect, a tree is vertical 'ground', full of good things to eat. They're living sky-scraper hotels, with restaurants on every floor. A tree trunk may occupy a square metre of the garden but it provides a thousand cubic metres of surfaces in the air.

CREATING YOUR OWN WOODLAND GLADE

A woodland glade or edge can easily be reproduced in a garden. Just a few square metres of space is enough to establish a rich and diverse habitat that will attract animals, birds and insects galore. Since lots of garden animals hail from the woods, you will be giving them a home from home. And in spring you will have a proud parade of bluebells, snowdrops and wood anemones. Even one tree on a lawn, underplanted with woodland or hedgerow flowers, and with a creeper growing up its trunk, is of benefit to wildlife.

Tip: See what trees and shrubs your neighbours have planted and what trees grow locally. By creating a woodland that is similar to others in your area, wildlife will be able to migrate from garden to garden.

PLANNING AND ESTABLISHING

The crucial feature of the woodland edge is that it is comprised of several heights or storeys; the more layers you have the more species you will attract. Heights should increase or 'step up' from the front of the glade to the back in order to allow in as much light as possible. Think in terms of a three-tier system: the front or bottom tier is woodland shrubs; the middle or second layer is small trees; the back or third layer is large trees. In a small garden only two layers are planted – the small trees become the top canopy and the shrubs become the underplanting.

When planning the woodland glade, remember it should face the sunniest direction, so as to minimise the shadow cast over the rest of the garden. You should also consult your neighbours if the proposed glade is likely to throw shadow across their patch.

Trees are the staple of any woodland planting. The native oak is wildlife king, supporting 284 insect species and 600 species in all; the foreign horse chestnut supports just four insect species. Aside from silver birch and hawthorn already mentioned, rowan and crab apple are small trees with big wildlife potential. However, always retain any older existing broad-leaved trees in the garden, whether they be native or imported. Many insect and bird species are reliant on the cracked and holed bark.

Start the woodland edge by selecting and planting the trees. Keep the soil around them clear with leaf litter, which will also maximise soil moisture while they establish.

Next add shrubs and plants that enjoy dappled shade.

Good shrubs beneath the tree canopy are dog rose and bramble. Herbaceous plants and bulbs for the base attract insects as well as provide ground cover for smaller animals.

Put up bird and bat boxes, and encourage woodland creatures with a log or brush pile.

STEP-BY-STEP: HOW TO PLANT TREES

Evergreens should be planted in early autumn or late spring; deciduous trees should be planted in early winter. Trees and shrubs grown in containers can be planted at any time during the year when the ground is soft and moist. Never let bare-rooted stock dry out, and plant as soon as possible. If the ground is water-logged or frozen, plant temporarily in compost at a 45-degree angle (heeling in) and keep moist.

Step 1. When you come to final planting, dig a square hole, and if the tree is likely to suffer competition remove turf and weeds for a radius of 75cm from centre of hole.

Step 2. Tease out the tree's roots and plant in the hole. Do not incorporate organic additives since the roots eat this in preference to spreading out into surrounding soil – the so-called 'corkscrew effect'.

Step 3. Backfill with excavated soil and firm with your heel to remove air pockets.

Step 4. Large trees and shrubs require staking; drive in this stake at a 45-degree angle across the face of the trunk to avoid roots, and secure tree with a tie.

> **Tip:** Once the upper storey is strong and high enough, grow some climbers up into the branches. Clematis and honeysuckle (*Lonicera periclymenum*) are suitable candidates.

TOP TEN TREES FOR A GARDEN OR WOODLAND EDGE

To find out which trees are suitable for your garden, take a look at what is growing in the local woods. This is one occasion where you should always plant native species, and broad-leaved species invariably support more biodiversity than conifers.

When planting trees, be aware that tree roots spread horizontally, so keep them away from house and shed walls.

Large (30m+ height)
Oak *Quercus robur* or *Quercus petraea*
Small-leaved lime *Tilia cordata*

Medium trees (15–30m in height)
Field maple *Acer Campestre*
Rowan *Sorbus aucuparia*
Silver birch *Betula pendula*

Small trees (less than 15m in height)
Hazel *Corylus avellana*
Hawthorn *Crataegus monogyna* or *Crataegus laevigata*
Crab apple *Malus sylvestris*
Bird cherry *Prunus padus*
Goat willow *Salix caprea*

TOP TEN PLANTS FOR A FLOWERING WOODLAND EDGE

Wood anemone *Anemone nemorosa*
Bugle *Ajuga reptans*
Foxglove *Digitalis purpurea*
Red campion *Silene dioica*
English bluebell *Hyacinthoides non-scripta*
Wood betony *Stachys officinalis*
Ox-eye daisy *Leucanthemum vulgare*

Stinking hellebore *Helleborus foetidus*
Common dog violet *Viola riviana*
Primrose *Primula vulgaris*

Also consider: lesser celandine (*Ranunculus ficaria*), lily of the valley (*Convallaria majalis*), wood cranesbill (*Geranium sylvaticum*), wood forget-me-not (*Myosotis sylvatica*).

MAINTAINING

Never was the motto 'Less is Best' more appropriate than in a woodland glade. Don't be tempted to constantly tidy – rotting leaves and branches are food sources and habitats for thousands of species of organism. Leaf litter is an excellent habitat for slugs, beetles and worms – all favourite meals for birds and hedgehogs. Only remove dead trees if they are dangerous. Don't pick up fallen fruit. If you must tidy, stack deadwood in piles, and put fallen autumn leaves in plastic sacks (holed for ventilation) to make leaf mould. The woodland edge is marvellously low maintenance gardening.

A few years after your trees have become established, you might want to consider the traditional woodland practice of coppicing. This involves cutting all stems down to just above ground level every few years, which prevents the canopy from becoming too crowded to let in light. The cut sticks are useful for the vegetable garden. Hazel, ash, alder, field maple, beech and hornbeam are commonly coppiced species.

A CHECKLIST OF TREES AND SHRUBS, AND THEIR USES IN THE WILDLIFE GARDEN

Alder *Alnus glutinosa*
Seeds popular with siskins, finches and other birds.

Alder buckthorn *Frangula alnus*
Food plant for brimstone butterfly larvae; berries for birds.

Ash *Fraxinus excelsior*
Keys (seeds) eaten by small mammals and birds.

Beech *Fagus sylvatica*
Seeds for birds and small mammals and birds. Attracts insects.

Bird cherry *Prunus padus*
Flowers attractive to insects; berries for birds and small mammals.

Blackberry *Rubus fruticosus*
Rich source of nectar for insects, with berries for birds, the common lizard, small mammals and also, surprisingly, mammals as big as the fox and badger. Good nesting cover too.

Blackthorn *Prunus spinosa*
Berries (sloes) for birds; flowers early source of nectar. Good, prickly cover for nesting birds.

Buckthorn *Rhamnus Cathartica*
Host plant for brimstone butterfly caterpillar.

Bullace *Prunus domestica* subsp. *Insititia* Also known as **wild plum**
Has many of the same wildlife virtues as blackthorn. The fruit is eminently edible by humans. Bullace vodka and bullace liqueur are favourite tipples of bullace cognoscenti.

Crab apple *Malus sylvestris*
Fruit eaten by birds and small mammals. For added wildlife value plant mistletoe in the bark to provide berries for birds in late winter.

Dog rose *Rosa canina*
Fruit (hips) for birds and small mammals. Good nesting site for birds.

Elderberry *Sambucus nigra*
Nectar and berries. Nest site for birds.

Field maple *Acer campestre*
Fruit eaten by small mammals; flowers attractive to insects.

Gean *Prunus avium* Also known as **wild cherry**
Fruit for birds.

Goat willow *Salix Caprea*
Teems with insects.

Gorse *Ulex europaeus*
Nesting cover for birds.

Guelder rose *Vihurnum opulus*
Nectar for insects, particularly hoverflies. Fruit for birds and small mammals, including the wood mouse.

Hawthorn *Crataegus monogyna*
Nectar; hips food source for thrushes, fieldfares, redwings; leaves for moth larvae including the magpie moth. Dense specimens provide nest sites for birds.

Hazel *Corylus avellana*
Hazelnuts food source for birds and small mammals.

Holly *Ilex aquifolium*
Fruit popular with thrushes. Foliage gives early nesting sites, and all year roosting. Host to holly blue butterfly.

Hornbeam *Carpinus betulus*
Seeds for birds.

Lime *Tilia cordata*
Flowers attract insects, particularly bees. Useful nesting tree.

Oak *Quercus robur* & *Quercus petraea*
Most important tree for wildlife, supporting 600 species in all. Excellent as food plant for insects, particularly moths, in turn making it top choice with insect-eating birds. Acorns food source for birds and mammals alike.

Red mulberry *Morus rubra*
Produces berries throughout the summer which are eaten by forty species of bird.

Rowan *Sorbus aucuparia*
Nectar-rich flowers attract insects in spring; bright-red fruits eaten by birds especially thrushes.

Scots pine *Pinus sylvestris*
Best conifer for wildlife; source of insects and site for nesting birds. Owls nest in the dense crowns.

Silver birch *Betula pendula*
Host to many insects, including moth larvae, thus also to insect-eating birds. Catkins also good source of food for birds.

Southern beech *Nothofagus*
Large, fast growing tree which is home to numerous birds and mammals (including bats), while others visit for the autumn nuts.

Spindle *Euonymus europaeus*
Nectar for insects; fruit for birds. Does best on chalk and limestone soils.

Sweet briar *Rosa rubiginosa*
Hips are a food source for small mammals and birds. Good nesting cover.

Wayfaring tree *Viburnum lantana*
Berries for birds; flowers for insects.

Whitebeam *Sorbus Aria*
Flowers attract insects; fruit eaten by birds.

Wild privet *Ligustrum vulgare*
Birds nest in dense innards, and feed on fruit. Flowers attract insects.

Wild service tree *Sorbus torminalis* Also known as the **chequer tree**, after which the British Prime Minister's country residence is named. Source of nectar; fruits eaten by birds.

> **Tip:** To check out the extraordinary world of insects in trees and bushes, place an upturned umbrella or bed sheet underneath a shrub bush or small tree – and shake. In the avalanche of insects, look out for caterpillars disguised as twigs. These are called 'geometrids', from the Greek for 'ground' and 'measure', because their strange looping walk looks as though they are measuring the earth. Never touch caterpillars, especially hairy ones, unless you are wearing rubber gloves, as some have hairs that irritate the human skin. The hawthorn shield bug is one of the handsomest bugs around, green and reddish, and at 1.5cm in length hard to miss.

WILDLIFE TO WATCH OUT FOR

Great spotted woodpecker
This striking bird is one of the success stories of garden wildlife, with its numbers up by 50 per cent in a decade.

The signature 'drumming' of woodpeckers is the means by which they mark out territory in early spring as well as prise invertebrates from wood. Woodpeckers flock to feeders, where their long tongues – which protrude 4cm beyond the bill – can reach almost any morsel. Look out for great spotted woodpeckers especially in June and July, when adults escort the young into gardens to show them the best feeding places.

Great spotted woodpeckers are easily distinguished from Britain's other pied woodpecker, the lesser spotted, by their size. The great is the size of a starling, the lesser the size of a greenfinch.

Wood mouse

Undoubtedly the commonest mammal in the British garden, the wood mouse has penetrated even into inner city areas. Mainly nocturnal, the wood mouse is an agile climber and can bound kangaroo-like to avoid predators. If caught, it can shed its tail. Nonetheless it is the stock food of foxes, cats and birds of prey. The wood mouse's life expectancy is just 12–20 months.

The wood mouse has cartoonishly large ears and eyes; the house mouse, with which it is sometimes confused, does not.

CHAPTER 6
FENCES AND HEDGES

The boundary with the neighbours is hell and heaven for wildlife. The ubiquitous wooden panel fence can act as a prison wall for mammals, and is certainly implicated in the decline of the hedgehog – it prevents Mrs Tiggy-Winkle being able to roam from garden to garden in search of supper. Wooden panel fences can be a vertical desert, as can brick and stone walls that are flawlessly maintained.

Fortunately, nothing is easier than greening a fence or wall to make it more appealing to wildlife. And quite possibly to you too.

If you already have a brick or stone wall, discuss with your neighbours the removal of a small section at the base for hedgehogs and other small mammal traffic. Then grow plants in gaps between the bricks or stones. Where there are no gaps, make some in the mortar and plant ivy-leaved toadflax (*Cymbalaria muralis*) and herb robert (*Geranium robertianum*), two plants which will enliven the dullest wall. Navelwort (*Umbilicus rupestris*) will grow on almost any rocky-bricky surface, as will the tough little succulent biting stonecrop (*Sedum acre*). Moss and lichens, both of which will harbour and feed insects, can be encouraged with the same trick used on roofs, a quick painting with diluted natural yogurt. Ferns will find the cracks for themselves.

Then grow a native climber such as ivy over the wall. Climbers are also an obvious solution for greening wooden and chain-link fences too.

FENCES

Sometimes, for reasons of space, economy or lack of soil, only a mass-produced fence of overlapping softwood planks will do. But do not despair; the overlapping planks make an unacknowledged wildlife habitat. Take a look at any such fence a year or two in age and where the panels overlap there are sure to be the pupae of butterflies and moths, spiders' nests, clusters of hibernating ladybirds and shoals of running earwigs.

What kills the fence as a habitat is creosote and preservative. But, naturally enough, you want your fence to last. A compromise is to treat the fence with a wood treatment product when the fence is first erected – and then leave it alone. To prettify the drab fence, consider leaving the uprights sticking 30cm or so above the fence and fixing prefabricated trellis between them – this will enable climbers to spread along. As well as providing support for the climbers, the trellis panels will create additional space for nesting birds and hibernating insects.

Support for climbers can also be made by attaching heavy gauge wires horizontally from post to post. Aside from ivy (*Hedera*), winter jasmine (*Jasminum nudiflorum*), dog rose (*Rosa canina*) and *Clematis* can all enhance the dullest, most barren fence. So can the underestimated hop (*Humulus*), that giver of intoxicating, sharp fragrance in late summer, and supplier of green shoots for lunch in spring.

Be aware that fixing trellis does add to the instability of the fence; the supporting posts should be at least 60cm into the ground.

The greening of fences can also be achieved by growing more-or-less free-standing shrubs in front of them. *Cotoneaster horizontalis* is top class in this category, as it requires little tying on – bees are grateful for its flowers in spring and birds love the winter berries.

Tip: Do ask about the fence's environmental credentials. Timber marked Forest Stewardship Council indicates that it has come from sustainably managed woodland.

Don't let fencing drive you up the wall. Wooden-panel fencing is far from being the only fencing on the market. Hand-crafted traditional and rustic fencing are widely available. Woven fences made from split hazel, oak laths and willow wands look rustic and 'naturalistic', and may suit the style of your garden better.

Tip: Everything you do to green a fence with climbers can also green a house wall – fix prefab trellis onto battens which leave a gap for birds to nest behind. Fixing nest boxes to the upright also gives additional 'wildlife value'. Put blue tit boxes near the top, and robin and wren boxes a little lower down.

HEDGEROWS

Half of Britain's rural hedges have been lost in the last fifty years. These lost hedges were more, much more, than simple boundaries. They were cover for nesting and roosting birds, homes for insects and small mammals, their flowers and fruits foodstuff for faunal multitudes. They were also a 'green corridor' allowing animals to move safely from place to place.

Planting a hedge makes sense for a gardener for reasons other than its 'wildlife value'. A hedge has a lower installation cost than fencing, is better at resisting high winds, is superb at keeping out burglars when prickly (some two-thirds of burglars enter properties via the back garden), is easier to shape around curves and reduces noise. A hedge changes with the seasons, and is infinitely more attractive than almost any utility fencing. The only downside is that they do take time to grow.

STEP-BY-STEP: PLANTING A WILDLIFE HEDGE

Indisputably, the best wildlife hedges mix four or five native species that provide flowers and berries for food, together with nesting sites and year-round cover. There should also be space at the base for underplanting with wildflowers. A good native hedge is really a woodland edge on a small scale.

But against the needs of wildlife, you must balance your own needs. Does the hedge need to keep out vandals? Hide an eyesore? Do you want it to tone with the house, the neighbourhood? The answers will affect your choice. You might well find that a single-species hedge is right for you, if only because it is easier to maintain than mixed hedge.

To a large degree any hedge has wildlife potential. Even a conifer can be a snug roosting site for birds and a hibernation hotel for insects. And a corridor which a pipistrelle bat can hawk along and feel safe from predators bigger than he or she.

Step 1. In the autumn, clear the area to be planted and dig a trench 60cm wide and 30cm deep. Refill, but as you do, mix in oodles of organic compost plus fertiliser at rate of 50g per m². Bone, fish and blood are all perfect. Leave to settle for a week.

Step 2. Rake over the trench, then consolidate the ground by walking over it in your wellies to remove large air pockets and fissures. Gently rake level.

Step 3. Hedging is best planted in two rows. Use pegs and garden twine to mark out two lines about 30cm apart, along which the young hedging plants (whips) are to be planted.

Step 4. Using a spade, make a narrow planting pit, slide the roots of the whip into the prised-apart hole. Withdraw spade.

Step 5. Using the heel of a boot, make sure the plant is firm in the ground. But *do not leave a depression around the base of the plant –* water will accumulate. Instead, scrape up some earth so there is a slight mound around the plant's base.

Step 6. To protect the stems from rabbits, place guards around them.

When the hedge is established, do not forget to plant woodland and hedgerow plants underneath it. By the same token, any established hedge you inherit can be enhanced with judicious planting of wildflowers. Species to try include primrose (*Primula vulgaris*), wild strawberry (*Fragaria vesca*), foxglove (*Digitalis*), campion (*Silene*), herb robert (*Geranium robertianum*), stitchwort (*Stellaria*) and violet (*Viola reichenbachiana*).

TOP TEN NATIVE HEDGING PLANTS

Beech *Fagus sylvatica*
A deciduous tree that gives screening almost the year round because it retains its dead leaves through winter. It's happiest on alkaline soils but will tolerate pretty much anything. Beech nuts (mast) are foodstuff for numerous small mammals as well as finches. The leaves provide a meal for the caterpillars of twenty moth species, including the large emerald.

Spindle *Euonymus europaeus*
Good for dry, chalky and limestone soils, and windswept sites. Seems far too exotic to be British: the seed pods, which are cherry-pink, split open to reveal day-glo orange seeds which are eaten by several bird species. The whole shrub colours interestingly in its autumn dieback.

Blackthorn *Prunus spinosa*
With talons up to 30mm long, blackthorn is ideal for keeping burglars at bay. A mass of bloom in March gives nectar to early bees and other pollinators, its leaves are the food of numerous caterpillars, and birds love its autumn fruit, the globose sloe. The same fruits, if the thrush family will spare some, make the wildlife

gardener's alcoholic pick-me-up: sloe gin. Just mash or prick sloes with a fork, put into a sweet jar (or similar), oodle in 0.5kg white sugar and fill with gin. Shake once a day for two months. Drink sparingly! Blackthorn supports over 150 species of wildlife, excluding humans.

Hawthorn *Crataegus monogyna*

A must-have. Hawthorn is the traditional stock-proof fence of farmland, and the same virtue of thorny thickness makes it hugely attractive to nesting birds. One of the first trees to blossom in spring, the 'May' produces early nectar for all manner of bugs. The berries (haws) are food for rodents and, especially, migrating winter birds, and may well attract redwings and fieldfares into the garden. Overall, hawthorn can host as many as 150 insect species, among them the magpie moth, whose caterpillars feed on the leaves. Look out for the crab apple spider, which hides in the blossom and nabs passing insects.

Holly *Ilex aquifolium*

Everybody's favourite evergreen. Gives shelter, nesting sites and food for numerous small perching birds, among them robins and hedge sparrows. Only female holly bushes produce berries; if there are no male trees nearby you will have to plant one to act as a pollinator in order to get said berries.

Dog rose *Rosa canina*

'Dog' is a corruption of 'dag' or dagger, in honour of the plant's thorns. Hips, the plant's autumn fruits, are a valuable food resource for migrating and indigenous birds. The seeds inside make itching powder too. A floral definition of Britain, it's what Rupert Brooke was referring to in the poem 'The Old Vicarage, Grantchester', when he wrote the couplet 'Unkempt about those hedges blows/An English unofficial rose'.

Alder buckthorn *Rhamnus frangula*

A denizen of damp soil. Produces nectar-rich flowers, which become red then black wildlife-friendly berries. Thornless.

Hornbeam *Carpinus betulus*

The small autumn nuts are eaten by a wide variety of birds and mammals, and rabbits and mice sometimes gorge on the new leaves. The hornbeam is also the host plant for the copper underwing moth. For gardeners and roosting birds alike, the tree has the great advantage of retaining its withered brown leaves over winter.

Yew *Taxus baccata*

Slow-growing evergreen of improbable longevity; some specimens are 4,000 years old. Sports berries eaten by waxwings, thrushes and other birds. The tree is host to several moth species, including the willow beauty.

Wayfaring tree *Viburnum lantana*

Native to chalk and limestone soils, this attractive shrub produces clusters of scented white flowers in late spring, which are succeeded by masses of bright red berries in autumn that fade to black.

Tip: Holly (*Ilex aquifolium*), blackthorn (*Prunus spinosa*), dog rose (*Rosa canina*) and hawthorn (*Crataegus monogyna*) are among the best native species for a burglar-unfriendly hedge; *Berberis* and *Pyracantha* are non-native species which are good for wildlife and bad for burglars. They can also both be trailed up drainpipes as a further deterrent to house-breakers.

WILDLIFE TO WATCH OUT FOR

Hedge sparrow

No less than thirty-four species of British bird commonly nest in hedges, the most typical of which is the hedge sparrow. Its name in Old English was 'hegesugge'. Today, it is called the dunnock, but it remains the little bird of the hedges. The sight of the hedge sparrow's sky-blue eggs huddled in a nest is one of the delights of the wildlife garden.

Woodlouse spider

Only a woodlouse spider could find a woodlouse spider attractive; flesh-coloured, with a bulbous abdomen and six eyes *Dysdera crocata* will never pass as a 'charismatic' garden animal. Look for this unappealing yet strangely beguiling arachnid at night, as it hunts through damp leaf litter in the bottom of the hedge in search of a woodlouse to eat. The prey is pierced by *Dysdera crocata*'s strong fangs – which are also strong enough to pierce human skin.

Robin's pincushion

Search through a hedge and you might find an intriguing, abnormal growth on a plant: a gall. Perhaps the most extraordinary of the hedgerow galls is the Robin's pincushion, which is caused by a tiny gall-wasp called *Diplolepis rosae*, and is found on the field rose and dog rose. The female wasp lays her eggs in the bud of the rose, and in so doing re-codes the normal process of flower growth to produce a round moss-like ball. By August the ball may have grown up to 7–10cm in diameter, and inside is a honeycomb of chambers in each of which is the grub of the wasp. Also in residence inside the gall is a motley community of opportunists, including other gall-wasps, plus parasitic wasps. There is even a species of chalcid wasp that parasitise parasitic wasps that parasitise parasitic wasps – in other words, a chain of four parasitic wasps feeding on each other.

Save-a-species: Hedgehog

Hedgehogs are the quintessential mammals of the hedgerow habitat, fossicking around the bottom for slugs, beetles and other invertebrates, and using its innermost recesses for hibernation in winter. In summertime, they will sometimes make a daytime nest in the hedge-bottom for a snooze.

Resident in Britain since the last Ice Age, the hedgehog has declined by as much as 25 per cent in ten years according to surveys by the People's Trust for Endangered Species. Their distinctive, trademark spiky coat contains about 5,000 spines, which can grow up to 2.5cm long; when the hedgehog rolls into a defensive ball the spines keep most predators at bay.

Gardens reproduce hedgehog habitat wonderfully – if they are chemical-free and have woody, shrubby cover and an area of long grass. Since hedgehogs wander as much as 2km a night they need 'corridors' to reach from one garden to the next. Although hedgehogs can climb surprisingly well, leave a hedgehog-sized hole at the end of the fence for them to enter and exit. When hedgehogs are climbing fences they are more liable to predation.

You are as likely to hear the nocturnal hedgehog as you are to see it. They locate their prey by smell, hence their constant snuffling, which sounds curiously human. In spring, hedgehog courtship is infamously noisy.

Hedgehogs hibernate. A compost heap, a log pile, a heap of leaves all make hibernaculums. You could even tempt hedgehogs with a hedgehog home (see page 148).

Hedgehogs get thirsty. A pond with shallow sides makes an ideal watering hole. Otherwise leave a bowl of water out for *Erinaceus europaeus*, but never milk, as this seems to cause gastroenteritis. Hedgehogs sometimes 'wake up' during winter months to take food and water before returning to hibernation. Dried cat food, sunflower seeds or mealworms, placed in a dish under an upturned washing-up bowl with the entrance cut out, make good snacks.

DRY STONE WALLS

Mortarless dry stone walls are meccas for wildlife because of all of their nooks and crannies. Near innumerable species of insect, spider and invertebrate will live in the recesses, together with reptiles, rodents and birds. They're a magnificent micro-habitat.

Dry stone walls look easy to build. Alas, they are not. If you do want to go down the DIY dry stone wall route you might want to attend a course (The Conservation Volunteers and the Dry Stone Walling Association run courses), or be shown the tricks of the trade by an experienced dry stone waller – this endangered species is still found in the great dry stone wall regions like the Dales and Cotswolds.

The alternative for the rest of us is to make a rockery (see the next chapter) or a mini replica dry stone wall as a garden feature. One great advantage of a mini stone wall is that it does not need to be laid perfectly; indeed a slight 'tumbling down' effect gives a pleasing impression of antiquity, as well as making a useful animal haven. Our tumbling down wall is next to the gate to the herb garden, suggesting it is Ye Olde Pathe rather than Ye Goode Idea Last Yeare.

DO-IN-A-DAY: MAKE A MINI DRY STONE WALL

To be useful as a wildlife micro-habitat, a mini stone wall has to be 1m or more in length.

- Excavate a trench a metre or more in length to a depth of 10cm. Width is key, because you need to provide dark passages and chambers so the wall needs to be at least 30cm wide.
- Now stack the stone as neatly as you can in two exterior walls with a gap between them. Put the larger stones on the bottom and try to taper the wall inwards slightly as you build upwards to the height of 1m. (That is, the top should be narrower than

the bottom of the wall.) Any taller than 1m and you start to run into problems where the wall begins to lean and might collapse.

- Lichen will soon establish itself on the wall, and the narrow crevices will soon collect wind-blown dirt. Mosses will follow. And after moss come ferns and flowers.
- For those impatient with nature taking its course, you can fast-forward the process of colonisation by stuffing some – not all – of the gaps with soil into which have been sprinkled native wildflower seeds. Or introduce a small number of plants that will self-seed.
- For the tops of walls, the succulent biting stonecrop (*Sedum acre*) is a stalwart, and the pretty flowers of maiden pink (*Dianthus deltoides*) love a view. As the Latin name of thrift (*Armeria maritima*) suggests, it is a seaside cliff-dweller by nature, and will therefore happily sit atop a wall, which is an altogether more comfortable berth. As we have seen already, navelwort (*Umbilicus rupestris*), and ivy-leaved toadflax (*Cymbalaria muralis*) will perch in the unlikeliest crevices.

CHAPTER 7
ROCKERIES AND
COASTAL GARDENS

Along with avocado-coloured bathroom suites and space hoppers, rockeries seem to belong to the 1970s, and are the depth of garden fashion. This is unfortunate, since a well-designed rockery can be an attractive use of a bank or slope, or a rockery can be used to give height to a flat garden. A rockery can certainly be a haven for wildlife.

In essence, a rockery is a mini cliff face and so will delight reptiles and other wildlife adapted to living in a specialised environment of dry, poor thin soil. Rockeries are an ideal habitat for those important and tireless pollinators, mason bees.

As a rule of thumb, the dimensions when designing a rockery should be that for every 30cm in height the rockery should be 2.5m–3m wide. There are no great rules about what direction a rockery should face; there are oodles of plants suitable for sun-drenched and shaded locations alike. About half of each rock should be set into the ground so it acts as a stable retaining wall for the soil behind. Think a series of stepped terraces with the rocks making the 'front walls'.

What made the rockery fall out of gardening vogue was the tendency for them to be constructed from large, regimented stones (invariably from limestone quarries). To achieve a more natural look try to source local stone, in somewhat varied sizes, and then replicate real geological features. Natural rock formations do not have uniform vertical cracks with uniform horizontal fissures. A rockery is not a brick wall. It is also vital that you have a basic idea of the planting scheme of your rockery and leave planting pockets in the rocks accordingly.

To make the rockery friendly to wildlife, leave some crevices between the stones for wildlife to colonise. Diversity in size of the gaps will maximise the variety of wildlife that will make the rockery home. You can prevent soil from washing out by making a small inner wall of stone some inches behind the main facing stones where appropriate.

A rockery sited next to a pond will give a refuge to amphibians, and quite possibly a hibernaculum.

Tip: Instead of buying stones, try to find unwanted ones. It saves money and is better for the environment. Farmers, road makers and house builders often have stone they have no use for. Recycling centres are another good source.

TOP TEN PLANTS FOR A WILDLIFE-FRIENDLY ROCKERY

Pinks *Dianthus*
Creeping thyme *Thymus serpyllum*
Rockery alyssum *Alyssum saxatile*
Bell heather *Erica cinerea*
Spirea *Spiraea Japonica Alpina*
Houseleek *Sempervivum*
Ivy-leaved toadflax *Cymbalaria muralis*
Red valerian *Centranthus ruber*
Wild strawberry *Fragaria vesca*
Harebell *Campanula rotundifolia*

WILDLIFE TO WATCH OUT FOR

Common lizard
The common lizard is the UK's most widespread and numerous reptile, and is the only reptile native to Ireland. Also known as the

viviparous lizard, the species is unusual among reptiles for giving birth to live young rather than laying eggs. They spend a lot of time basking in sun, to warm up enough to hunt, but always within reach of a bolt hole. Rockeries provide this. Their main prey consists of invertebrates such as insects, spiders, earthworms and snails.

A GRAVEL GARDEN

What could be worse for wildlife than gravel? Quite a lot actually. A gravel garden can be the wildlife-friendly solution to paths, off-street parking, barbecue pits, seating areas. Or maybe you just don't want to do much gardening, and require a low-maintenance area. Tarmac, concrete and wooden decking are the three great 'Nos' of the wildlife garden. If gravel can be used instead of any of these then it's a win for wildlife.

Gravel can be planted up and will naturally be colonised by flora and invertebrates. For the householder, gravel has the advantage of being easy to put down and easy to maintain. And it is cheap.

PROJECTS FOR SMALL SPACES: MAKE A GRAVEL GARDEN

- Mark out the shape of the area you want to gravel with a rope.
- To stop the gravel from 'travelling' you may need to put in edging. Timber planks treated with an environmentally friendly preservative are inexpensive and easy to lay.
- Dig out the garden to a depth of 5cm, and rake flat.
- If you do not require your plants to self-seed, lay landscape fabric over the soil before planting. Cut crosses in the fabric large enough to insert each rootball.
- Plant with suitable drought-resistant plants (see below).
- Mulch with 5cm gravel.
- Water well.

Gravel gardens are best suited to dry, low fertile soil. With 'clayey' soil, dig down to 8cm and remove the soil. Replace 3cm of soil, mixing it with plenty of organic matter, and rake flat. Then lay down weed-resistant membrane, if desired, and plant as above.

There is, of course, no need to gravel a whole area. A path might be alternately paving slabs and gravel 'slabs', or off-road parking might be mostly paving slabs with attractive mini-gravel gardens between them.

Tip: Check any gravel you purchase is not from a marine source. Dredging damages marine ecosystems.

TOP TEN PLANTS FOR A GRAVEL GARDEN

Almost all drought-resistant plants from coast and heath will thrive in a gravel garden, especially these ten:

Cosmos *Cosmos sulphureus*
Easy to grow annual with a mass of vivid blooms.

Greater sea kale *Crambe cordifolia*
Herbaceous perennial growing to 1.8m, with branches of small, scented white flowers. A member of the cabbage family.

Jerusalem sage *Phlomis russeliana*
Herbaceous perennial from the Middle East. Good for bees.

Mullein *Verbascum olympicum*
Tall, bright yellow biennial/perennial. Bee friendly.

Chives *Allium schoenoprasum*
First class nectar-provider for bees. Useful in the kitchen.

Lavender *Lavandula angustifolia*
Familiar aromatic shrub, to which bees make a bee-line, as do butterflies. Seeds eaten by birds in autumn.

Catmint *Nepeta x faassenii*
Beloved by felines (hence the name), along with a range of insects. Delightful herbaceous perennial with lilac-blue flowers from May to September.

Thyme *Thymus vulgaris*
Neat, tough, an olfactory sensation, insect friendly and indispensable in the kitchen.

Hebe *Hebe salicifolia*
One of the taller of the hebe family, and can even be grown as a hedge. Thrives on well-drained alkaline soil, and is a popular destination for butterflies and bees.

Rock rose *Helianthemum nummularium*
An attractive evergreen shrub which provides shelter for all manner of creatures. The red flowers, which appear in spring, attract several species of insect.

THE COASTAL WILDLIFE GARDEN

Gardening on the coast can be tough. The soil is usually sandy, and sadly lacking in nutrients, while the constant salt-laden winds break plant limbs and 'burn' leaves. On the west coast the rainfall is, to use a euphemism, plentiful, while on the east coast it's often sparse.

Do not abandon hope. With the right plants a wealth of specially adapted wildlife can be encouraged into an attractive coastal garden.

PLANNING

There are two keys to successful wildlife gardening by the coast, and they both require working with nature.

Firstly, choose those plants that are suited to salt-drenched wind and free-draining soil. As a rule, plants with small, glossy or leathery leaves will make light of the harsh conditions. Plants which have *maritima* or *littoralis* in their Latin name are natural coastal dwellers. These include native, coastal plants for which your garden will be home from home, among them sea kale (*Crambe maritima*).

Secondly, give the garden shelter. Visiting wildlife will not want to be buffeted, and equally some seaside plants are adapted to living in those places protected from the wind. Plant suitable shrubs and trees as a windbreak: holly (*Ilex aquifolium*), holm oak (*Quercus ilex*), four-stamen tamarisk (*Tamarix tetrandra*), escallonia (*Escallonia* spp.) and New Zealand privet (*Griselinia littoralis*) all make handsome and effective hedges-cum-shelterbelts.

Or erect wind-filtering screens. Trellis and willow hurdles are a 'natural' screen, and polypropylene webbing is the unnatural but effective alternative. Solid dry stone walls are wonderful – unless they are situated where they will create turbulence, which will only exacerbate the problem of windiness in the garden. To prevent the erosion of poor soil by the wind, use plants with fibrous systems to stop the garden blowing away. Blue fescue (*Festuca glauca*) and onion grass (*Romulea rosea*) will serve you well.

MAINTAINING

Plants in the coastal garden will need feeding, especially when young. Handily, an organic and free fertiliser is likely within reach. Gather seaweed from the seashore and – after washing to remove the surface salt – dig straight into the soil.

Since poor soil quality and high salt levels cause moisture-loss, beds should be mulched. In very sandy soils, well-rotted manure should be dug in to conserve moisture.

Tip: Piled up driftwood makes an attractive feature, and an in-keeping log pile for small creatures.

TOP TEN PLANTS FOR A COASTAL GARDEN

Box-leaf azara *Azara microphylla*
Evergreen shrub, which produces vanilla-scented yellow flowers in spring.

Thrift 'Sea Pink' *Armeria maritima*
Evergreen perennial with pink flowers, common on sandy cliffs.

Sea buckthorn *Hippophae rhamnoides*
Native shrub which produces a mass of orange berries in summer.

Sea kale *Crambe maritima*
Hardy member of the cabbage family.

Sea holly *Eryngium maritimum*
Nectar from June to September, flowers attract bees, butterflies and beetles. An increasingly rare native species. To plant it would be to help conserve it.

Lamb's ears *Stachys byzantina*
Evergreen with woolly white foliage (thus the name) and pinky-purple flowers in summer.

Hummingbird fuchsia *Fuchsia magellanica*
Deciduous shrub, which produces small red flowers in summer. Does best in warmer climes.

Four-stamen tamarisk *Tamarix tetrandra*
A tall shrub up for a big challenge. Will tolerate salt, wind and poor soil – and still produce pink flowers in spring.

Bird's-foot trefoil *Lotus corniculatus*
Native species common on dry grassland, sand and shingle.

Yellow horned poppy *Glaucium flavum*
Striking native, yellow flowering plant which attracts bees and hoverflies for its pollen. The seed pods grow up to 30cm in length. Be aware that the sap is poisonous.

A GREEN ROOF

If you only have a small garden or no garden at all, perhaps you have a roof that could be made into a horticultural heaven for the birds and the bees and the butterflies? Many roofs can be 'greened'. A garage with a flat asphalt roof should be capable of supporting a lightweight living roof, as should a pitched garden shed if given a minimum of structural reinforcement. Outhouses, extensions and bike sheds might also offer possibilities. And don't forget Fido's kennel.

Living roofs are not just good for wildlife: they are good for the environment in numerous ways. In winter, they can provide insulation, in summer they can help cool down the room below. By acting as a 'sponge' they retain water and so reduce the likelihood of flash flooding. The types of green roof can vary greatly, but basically they are of three sorts:

Extensive
These are shallow, lightweight and easily maintained, and the most common living roofs. Since they use a growing medium of as little as 2cm they tend to dry out. Any plant living here needs to be tough. Wild coastal and mountain species such as the ice plant (*Sedum spectabile*) are recommended.

Semi-extensive

Designed to hold a greater depth of growing medium – 10–20cm – and therefore a more varied flora. It needs to be placed on a relatively strong structure. Mixtures of low or medium perennials, grasses, bulbs and annuals from dry habitats are suitable. It can also be turned into a chalkland-type wildflower meadow.

Intensive

These have very deep substrates allowing the growth of shrubs, even trees. Almost all intensive living roofs are purpose built; the cost of adapting an existing building to support the immense weight of the roof is invariably prohibitive.

Tip: The lightest living roofs – and the simplest to create – are those supporting lichens and mosses. Lichens are composite, symbiotic organisms made up of fungi (which dominate) and algae or cyanobacteria. Mosses are green plants that spread by spores. Both lichens and mosses provide habitats for thousands of microscopic animals as well as many invertebrates, which, in turn, are food for birds. Both mosses and lichens can be encouraged to grow on roofs. Firstly, make sure the roof is free of dust and loose debris. Then paint areas with a weak solution of natural yogurt. Mosses can be transplanted, but you would need to ask the permission of the landowner whose moss you are taking. Transplanted moss will need regular watering until established.

DO-IN-A-DAY: GREEN A GARDEN SHED ROOF

As garden sheds are generally lightweight structures, even an ice plant (*Sedum spectabile*) blanket is likely to require additional support. Take expert advice from a builder, carpenter, architect or structural engineer.

However, it should be possible to convert a garden shed with a felt roof with the minimum of outlay using materials available from a DIY store.

- Add extra structural support to the shed if required.
- Cover the existing felt roof with a waterproof membrane of 300 micron damp-proof polythene or butyl pond liner. The waterproof layer should be laid in one continuous sheet, otherwise the sheets should overlap by at least 20cm. Visqueen EcoMembrane, available from builders' merchants, is a damp-proof membrane made from 100 per cent post-use polyethylene.
- Then lay down a filter sheet. This allows water to drain off the roof but stops the escape of fine materials in the substrate.
- On top of the filter sheet goes a water-retaining moisture blanket. Commercial moisture blankets made of geotextile materials can be purchased from DIY stores. Otherwise use old woollen blankets, cardboard or towels.
- Using rot-proof timber, build a frame around the roof to contain the substrate on which your garden will grow. You will need to make sure the timber is deeper than the intended garden.
- Spread substrate on the roof. Aggregates such as limestone chippings, crushed brick, perlite, lica, sand, rockwool and gravel are the commonest substrates. A depth of 5–10cm is required.
- Add a thin 1cm layer of sand or subsoil.
- Drill holes in the retaining timber frame every 10cm for emergency drainage. The holes should be just above the level of the substrate.
- Plant up. Mat-forming species of moss, houseleeks (*Sempervivum*) and sedum (especially *S. album*, *S. acre*, *S. rupestre*) are recommended. Sedum is an excellent source of nectar.

Tip: You can cheat by buying readymade sedum matting or sedum tiles. These generally contain a mix of six or more sedum species. Suppliers include www.sedumgreenroof.co.uk and www.enviromat.co.uk.

CHAPTER 8
FRUIT AND VEGETABLE GARDENING

The likelihood is that you will have little problem attracting wildlife to the vegetable and fruit plot. Woodpigeons will eat your thoughtfully provided pea shoots, every slug and snail for a three-kilometre radius will munch your strawberries, and all the cabbage white caterpillars on earth will nibble your brassicas.

CREATING THE WILDLIFE-FRIENDLY FRUIT AND VEGETABLE GARDEN

A balance has to be struck between feeding yourself and feeding garden creatures.

- Give up the evil weed-killer, along with chemical pesticides. These inorganic chemical concoctions upset the natural balance and tend not to discriminate between pests and predators. In the fruit and vegetable garden the ideal is to encourage beneficial predators and let them do the pest-control for you. Think toads, song thrushes, hedgehogs, grass snakes, bats and beneficial insects like ladybirds. Predators need a home in the fruit and veg garden. Try making a bug hotel for ladybirds, a log pile for the common frog and a bat box for a pipistrelle.

- Improve soil conditions to grow strong and healthy plants which are more resistant to pests. The answer lies in the soil-improver compost (rather than in nitrogen fertilisers that cause the sort of sappy growth loved by pests).

- Always find out what sort of soil you have – it is acid or alkaline? – because trying to grow plants in an unsuitable environment stresses them and makes them more prone to disease and pest-infestation.

- Keep unwanted intruders out by putting up non-toxic barriers, such as nets over soft fruit and coarse bark (or sharp gravel, sand or wood ash) around the vegetable beds to deter slugs and snails. Copper wire is another slug-deterrent. But you might want to leave some of your soft fruit for birds to gorge on.

- Consider companion planting, the idea of which is that the companion plant either repels the pest from your crop or selflessly attracts the pest away to itself (see below). While there is no scientific evidence as to why companion planting works, it has been used for generations with success.

Most importantly, keep calm and carry on gardening. Changing to a non-chemical regime will have ups and downs until the edible garden finds a natural equilibrium. Realistically, you will have pest problems until you have sufficient predators. Be prepared to remove slugs and caterpillars by hand. Or invest in a pet duck. This will hoover up molluscs with gleeful abandon.

> **Tip:** Slugs are generally nocturnal, so go out at night with a torch and collect them. To kill them, either cut in half or cover with salt. Otherwise sink a container of beer into the ground. The slugs find beer impossible to resist, and will slither into this trap and drown.

COMPANION PLANTING

The idea of companion planting is to use combinations of plants to reduce pests. Some companion plants are so drop dead gorgeous to pests that they won't worry your produce; other companion plants are so whiffy they drive the pests away. Sometimes companion plants confer another benefit, such as improved vigour – growing beans creates nitrogen in the soil, which is used by other plants to grow. Companion planting is usually done in the vegetable patch, but there is no reason why it cannot be employed everywhere in the garden.

The general principles of companion planting are:
- Mix together fruit and vegetables, herbs and ornamental plants.
- Do not plant up a large area with the same type of plant – it just gives the pests a bigger target to home in on.
- Plant a wide variety of plants. Diversity is the key.

MAIN COMPANION PLANTS

Plant	Benefits	Why
Asparagus	Tomato	Kills nematode that damages tomato roots.
Chive	Carrot Tomato	Combats fungal disease. Keeps aphids away.
Dill	Cabbage family	Attracts beneficial wasps that prey on pests.
Garlic	Rose	Keeps aphids away.
Hyssop	Cabbage	Diverts cabbage white butterfly.
Leeks	Bean, pea, carrot, turnip	Repels carrot fly; aids growth.
Lettuce	Carrot, strawberry	Diverts slugs, snails and rabbits.
Marigold	Cabbage family, leek, potato, tomato, lettuce	Kills nematode, repels aphids and whitefly, diverts slugs, attracts hoverflies.

Plant	Benefits	Why
Mint	Cabbage	Repels cabbage white butterfly.
Nasturtium	Radish, cabbage, cucumber, bean	Attracts pest insects, especially cabbage white butterfly, flowers repel aphids and cucumber beetle.
Onion family	Carrot, beetroot, tomato, lettuce	Smell deters pests, especially carrot fly.
Parsley	Beans, carrot, asparagus	Improves vigour, repels insect pests.
Radish	Spinach	Attracts leaf miner away from crop.
Sage	Carrot, cabbage family	Scent repels insect pests.
Sweetcorn	Bean	Attracts beneficial insects that prey on pest species.
Thyme	Cabbage family	Repels cabbage moths.
Tomato	Asparagus	Protects against asparagus beetle.

Tip: Leave a wild patch of nettles in the garden. They make an excellent habitat, and are a host plant for butterflies and moths. Nettles can also easily be made into fertiliser.

- Pick the tops – as if you were picking tea in Ceylon, but with gloves.
- Immerse in bucket of water – you will need to weight them down.
- Leave for three to four weeks.
- Dilute until tea-coloured. Put in watering-can and spray on plants.

You can also turn your nettles into tea, soup and greens for the family. Alternatively, in a moist 'wild' corner, plant comfrey (*Symphytum grandiflorum*), which can be cut and added to the compost heap as a source of potassium. Comfrey also makes tea. The flowers are pink, tubular and nectar-rich. In the herbaceous border comfrey errs towards invasiveness.

COMPOST

Where there's muck there's riches. Of sorts. Compost is healthy for your soil, and for all the wildlife that grows in and on it. Compost makes an excellent mulch, adds nutrients, improves soil structure, encourages beneficial fungi, is free to produce and comes guilt free – it has no wasteful packaging and has zero 'fuel miles'. On the contrary, a 2002 study by the Waste and Resources Action Programme concluded that the only factor which significantly reduced waste sent to landfill was home composting.

Besides being one of the most unambiguously positive things any gardener can do to enrich their soil and reduce landfill, composting is a wildlife attractor in its own right. Besides the teeming decomposer organisms and saprophytes which undertake the recycling process, compost heaps shelter many small animals such as voles and mice, and sometimes some large ones too, including nesting slow worms and hedgehogs. All enjoy the heat released by decomposition, as well as having a built-in larder. Compost heaps are teeming with slugs, beetles and earthworms – all favourite hedgehog snacks.

HOW TO COMPOST

Commercially available bins retain warmth and moisture and, generally speaking, make good compost quickly. They are usually inexpensive, and some councils, in order to reduce landfill, sell them at bargain prices. A home-built version is easy to construct, but it does need to exclude rain, allow air in and moisture out, as well as retain some warmth. Any square box-shape with slats or gaps will do. Ours is made from two sides of corrugated iron (peppered with holes), and two sides of packing crates covered with wire netting. The top is a piece of old carpet. Generally the old-fashioned DIY compost box is easier for mammals and reptiles to access if they are seeking shelter or winter quarters.

An earth base allows both drainage and the compost to be in contact with the soil. If this is not possible, build on concrete but add shovelfuls of soil to the heap. What books do not generally tell you is that the heap might be colonised by wildlife you don't want: rats. So if you do build on soil, put a 50mm wire netting at the base. The holes are big enough to let shrews, mice and reptiles through but small enough to bar rats.

The art of composting lies in getting the balance of matter in the heap right; ideally up to 50 per cent should be soft green stuff (vegetable kitchen waste, weeds, grass clippings) and 50 per cent brown woody material (prunings, wood chippings, paper, dead leaves, cardboard, straw from pet bedding).

When and where green stuff is in short supply, an accelerator may be required. Numerous commercial ones exist; the cheap and organic alternative favoured by many male gardeners is to pee on the heap. Urine contains nitrogen and phosphates. (Female urine contains harmful hormones, however, so shouldn't be added.)When and where there is a dearth of brown waste, carbon will need to be added.

Turn the heap every month or so, because this adds air. A heap that is wet and compacted will compost slowly, if at all.

Ideally, material for the heap is added in one go. Most gardeners though add little and often, and it still works out okay.

Garden compost takes between six and twenty-four months to mature. Mature compost is unmistakable – it's dark brown, crumbly, soil-like, with a distinct aroma of Bonfire Night and autumn leaves.

Tip: Compost heap too dry and nothing rotting? This means not enough moisture and too much brown waste. Add green stuff (grass clippings are ideal), a commercial activator, male urine or a bucket of manure for every 15cm layer of compost, or sulphur of ammonia at 140g per 15cm layer of compost.

WILDLIFE TO WATCH OUT FOR

Bottom layer (Advanced decomposition)
Centipedes (which are beneficial predators), earthworms, brandling worms (a red worm, which in a compost heap eat their own weight in green matter each day).

Middle layer (Early decomposition)
Common toad (usually taking refuge, but sometimes hibernating), common newt, wood mouse, grass snakes, slow worms, hedgehogs, fungi.

Top layer (Fresh material)

The large black slug, the brown-lipped/banded snail, millipedes, fruit flies, harvestmen, rove beetles, garden birds and spiders. Look especially for wolf spiders, a spider that hunts down its prey rather than trapping it in a web. They are useful pest controllers for the gardener. The dreaded tarantula of southern Italy is a close relative.

Tip: Position the compost heap in a sunny out-of-the-way corner and plant a shrub or two beside it. Not only do the shrubs hide the heap, they allow animals to sneak in and out of the heap without being seen.

WHAT TO COMPOST? A CHECKLIST

- Almost any vegetable or garden waste. Greens rot quickly and provide the nitrogen and moisture a compost heap needs.
- Brown material, e.g. dead leaves, torn cardboard and paper. This is slower to rot, provides fibre and carbon, and creates pockets and channels to allow air to circulate. Composting is an aerobic activity.
- You can also compost human hair, bedding and manure from herbivorous pets, tea bags.
- Wood ash.

Retain some compost for your next heap. It will 'ginger' a new cycle of decomposition.

WHAT NOT TO COMPOST

- Dog and cat litter.
- Pernicious weeds, eg bindweed, couch grass.
- Eggshells if your soil is alkaline.

- Too much newspaper. Avoid paper with a great deal of coloured ink or glossy pages.
- Female urine. It contains hormones damaging to the ecology of the garden.
- Diseased plant material.
- Fish, meat or dairy products.
- Bread.
- Coal ash.

A mini-wormery

A wormery is a purpose-built composting house for brandling worms which can live happily in a small yard or on a balcony. The wormery turns kitchen waste into almost odourless liquid plant feed and compost. The liquid plant feed is available after a few weeks and the compost is ready for use after a few months. There are a number of commercial suppliers. A mini-wormery for the interest of children is easy to make:

- Cut the top off a two litre plastic soft-drink bottle.
- Fill with alternate 5cm layers of fine sand and garden soil.
- Place a layer of dry leaves on the top.
- Dig up some earthworms and put them into the wormery.
- Gently add a small amount of water so that the soil is moist.
- Cover the sides of the bottle with black paper to keep the worms dark.
- When you want to observe the worms and their efforts in pulling the leaves down into the soil, remove the paper. Replace when you have finished observing.
- Check the wormery every day to ensure it does not dry out. After about a week, the worms will need to be returned to the garden.

CHAPTER 9
SHELTERS, FEEDERS AND WATCHING WILDLIFE

LOG PILE

Once Britain was almost wholly covered in woodland, but today only threatened fragments remain. In the old woodland ecosystem deadwood played a crucial role. Rot, in short, was good.

As luck has it, deadwood is the easiest micro-habitat for a gardener to create. You can do absolutely nothing and do good. Watch branches fall off trees, leave them where they lie, and feel virtuous. Deadwood is home to hosts of species. If you cannot bear to have branches lying around or they are inconvenient, pile them up. If you don't have any branches or logs of your own, scavenge unwanted timber. Log piles are one of the few wildlife garden imperatives.

A pile of logs need not be an eyesore; indeed, stacked in a sheltered corner it need not be seen at all. A sheltered corner that is also damp and shady is *the* absolutely ideal location for a log pile. Otherwise, grow ivy, clematis and ferns over the pile, and these will both mask its appearance and provide shadow for the wildlife that lurks within.

Use any large logs, although hardwood species with bark still attached are best. Do not use treated wood of any sort.

Dig a depression of about 60cm to lay the bottom logs in. This helps keep them moist. Stack with the largest logs at the bottom and try to end up with a slightly sloping effect, so water will run off – you want the inside to be damp, not drowned. If there are whistling gaps between the logs, stop with twigs.

The pile need not be large, with twenty smallish logs quite sufficient. Gradually the rotting logs will be colonised by algae, mosses, fungi, which will provide a humid micro-climate. Wood-boring insects will follow, and in their train will come small reptiles and mammals.

One insect you'll be sure to attract is the woodlouse, whether it is the common rough woodlouse, the common shiny woodlouse or the pill woodlouse. We are so familiar with this family of insects that we sometimes fail to appreciate how extraordinary they are; their nearest relatives are crabs and lobsters. Woodlice are actually crustaceans that have adapted to terrestrial living; they need dampness because they still use gills for breathing. The gills are located on their legs. Eggs are transported around in a brood pouch which is kept moist, like a miniature aquarium. Pill woodlice can roll themselves into a tiny ball or 'pill'. In medieval England pill woodlice used to be swallowed live – as 'pills' to cure digestive illnesses.

Woodlice are an important part of the nutrient recycling process. Large colonies of them smell of urine, since they excrete ammonia. Where there are woodlice there will be dysdera, nocturnal spiders with six eyes, who feed on the little grey scuttling crustaceans. Do not be tempted to pick up dysderids. They have fangs strong enough to penetrate human skin, and inject a venom some people are allergic to.

The dark, rotting insides of a log pile are the human idea of Hades, but they are a wildlife Elysium. Queen bees quite often over-winter in the innermost recesses, and fungus gnats, mosquito-like flies, are a welcome food source for small birds such as wrens in winter. Log piles are also an important habitat for the stag beetle.

Of course, if you are chopping down a tree that will end up in a nature-friendly log pile, you might want to leave a decent stump, up to several feet high, to rot in situ. Such standing deadwood can also be easily recreated by 'planting' a long log vertically; use a log about 90cm in length, burying half of it in the ground. When you re-fill the hole, plant native flowers and plants on the disturbed earth to soften the fake stump's appearance. Primroses (*Primula vulgaris*) and bluebells (*Hyacinthoides non-scripta*) always help provide a 'natural' look. Drilling holes in the exposed section will provide pre-fab homes for solitary bees and other insects.

A very large log can be used as a garden seat, and is easily rolled back ever so slightly for children to glimpse the bugs and the beasties that dwell underneath. The same fauna will be ever so grateful if you replace their home just as it was.

Save-a-species: Stag beetle

The stag beetle is Britain's largest terrestrial beetle, reaching 8cm in length, and is so named because of the male's fearsome 'jaws' which look like a stag's antlers. (The 'jaws' are actually no such thing; they are ornaments intended to attract a mate.) They are now rare in the UK, and possibly extinct in some Western European countries. They spend about five years as white grubs underground and emerge as fully grown adult insects in May and June. The eggs are always laid near to stumps or logs, showing the importance of a garden log pile.

Beetles and bugs are crucial to the eco-system. They are pollinators, decomposers and predators. There are over 4,000 species of beetle in Britain, many of which can be found in gardens.

Always cover water butts. Stag beetles are world class at getting into water butts, but village idiots at getting out and consequently drown.

BRUSH PILE

Similar to a log pile, but using twigs. The lack of big-diameter wood means that wood-boring insects and some fungi will not be attracted. On the other hand, the prunings which make the brush pile are easy to come by, whereas logs are not, unless you open your wallet.

Lay the twigs/prunings lengthways in a very shallow (2–3cm) depression, occasionally inserting twigs crossways to create air gaps. It does not matter whether the leaves are left on or not. Every year when you do your hedge-cutting or pruning, lay the cut twigs on top. A brush pile is a great way of using up trimmings. As well as harbourage for spiders, insects and other invertebrates, brush piles are shelter for small birds, reptiles and mammals.

CORRUGATED IRON, SLABS AND BOARDS

Gertrude Jekyll, Rosemary Verey and Vita Sackville-West would not approve. A sheet of corrugated iron is not beautiful, and in no way adds to the aesthetics of a garden. A sheet of corrugated iron is plain ugly ... unless you happen to be a snake, a slow worm or a lizard, when it is certain to be your idea of a modern des-res. Apart from a rock pile, nothing is more likely to attract reptiles to live in your garden. Position somewhere warm and bright, and paint half of the top black to quickly absorb heat. Not only will reptiles live underneath the monstrously ugly corrugated iron, they will lie on top in the belief that it is a sun terrace.

Doubtless, pop-eyed voles and shrews will be attracted to chez corrugated iron too, meaning the reptiles will have a full larder.

A quite different micro-habitat can be achieved by putting a large square slab or large board in a damp corner, where it may be colonised by frogs, toads and newts, especially if it is near water. You can now buy 'wildlife-friendly' concrete slabs which have built-in shelters; alternatively, if slabs are used for pathways, they can be laid for the same effect. Simply scoop out a small hollow trough about 4cm wide and 2cm deep in the base material you are laying the slabs on; this should reach from near the centre to the outside edge. When the slab is laid there is an instant roofed chamber where stability is not affected.

ROCK PILE

A simple pile of rocks is an almost instant habitat. Essentially, a rock pile is, like a dry stone wall or a rockery, a faux cliff face and if situated somewhere sunny will attract creatures that like it hot and dry. Lizards and snakes, for example. A quite different range of animals can be lured into your garden if the pile of stones is positioned somewhere shady, such as under a hedge or by a pond. Then, with luck, you will have among the visitors newts wanting to stay over for the winter.

Any rocks or bricks will do, as long as there is a variation in size. Something rather Turner Prize-like can be constructed with thought and inspiration, although the garden fauna is unlikely to care about its looks as long as there are plenty of cracks and recesses to hide away in. Obtaining stone should be easy. There can barely be a street in Britain without a skip bulging with bricks from home improvements, and other gardeners may well be trying to divest themselves of stones dug up from flower borders and vegetable patches. Local stone blends best; a pile of seaside-type stones purchased from a garden centre make a Zen-like modernist statement if you tend that way.

An hour or two's labour should be enough to make a rocky mini-hotel for reptiles, insects, birds and ground-dwelling mammals. Look out for the common lizard, wrens (which sometimes nest *very* low down), field voles and red-tailed bumblebees.

> **Tip:** Plant creeping thyme (*Thymus serpyllum*) over the rock pile. The plentiful nectar of this creeping herb attracts a wide range of insects, and you can filch some for cooking.

LACEWING HOTEL

There are about forty species of lacewing in Britain, one of which, the green lacewing, over-winters as an adult. Since the larvae of lacewings are enthusiastic predators of aphids, they are widely welcomed by gardeners. A single green lacewing will eat up to 10,000 aphids in its larval phase.

A shelter for these beneficial insects is simplicity itself.

- Cut the base off a plastic drink bottle, leaving the lid on to prevent water getting in.
- With a hole punch, make two small holes, one at each side of the base of the bottle.
- Cut a length of corrugated cardboard to fit the height of the bottle, leaving a 1cm gap at the bottom. Roll it up and place inside.
- Place straw between the gaps between the cardboard roll, but don't pack too tightly.
- Push a piece of string or thin wire through the holes at the base, to keep the cardboard in place.
- Tie string around the neck of the bottle to form a loop. Hang the hotel from branches of trees, shrubs or against fences at about the head height of an adult and preferably with foliage around it. Adult lacewings are attracted by lights, so place the hotels near house windows or exterior lights.

Put the lacewing hotels in place by the middle of August, which is when the insects start looking for winter quarters. If you have a lacewing hotel, it is important to remember to clean it out each year before August, because earwigs sometimes take up residence and will kill any lacewings as they arrive.

BAT BOXES

They suck blood and get tangled in your hair … Actually, only bats in far-off places suck blood, and if a bat can wing in and out of the telephone wires it can avoid your head. What bats really do is eat up to 3,000 insects each per night shift, a fair proportion of which in summertime are midges and mosquitoes. If nothing else, think of bats as flying insect-killers, making the garden nice to sit in. They are also a recognised indicator of biodiversity. Their presence is a sure sign of a healthy insect population.

There are seventeen species of bat in Britain, almost all of which have been recorded as being present in gardens. This is small surprise: as bats' natural breeding, roosting and feeding grounds have been lost under houses, roads and agri-business over the last fifty years, the garden has become an increasingly important refuge for these flying mammals.

And they are not blind, although they do generally rely on echo-location to 'see'.

HOW TO ATTRACT BATS TO THE GARDEN

The best way to do this is to create conditions which boost provision of their prey: flying insects. Try building a rock pile, brush pile, log pile, 'wildlife hotel' (below), wildflower lawn, hedge, compost heap and a pond. A border, bed or tub with night-scented flowers will attract moths for bats to feast on, as well as fill your garden with wondrous fragrances. Honeysuckle (*Lonicera periclymenum*), night-scented stock (*Matthiola bicornis*), evening primrose (*Oenothera biennis*), sweet rocket (*Hesperis matronalis*), night-scented catchfly (*Silene noctiflora*), and white jasmine (*Jasminum officinale*) are all excellent. Pale flowers are easier for nocturnal insects to find.

It almost goes without saying that stopping the use of pesticides is a bat-friendly measure.

Since bats loathe open spaces – about 10 per cent of bats are eaten by birds of prey – planting a tree, or several, will offer protective cover and help establish a corridor for them to fly along. In years to come, the tree might even become a bat roost.

A somewhat quicker way of giving a bat a home is to make a bat box.

MAKE YOUR OWN BAT BOX

Bat boxes are artificial roosts and breeding sites, standardly made of wood or woodcrete (a mixture of wood chips and concrete), which provide bats with alternatives to their natural roosts in trees and tumble-down buildings. Bat boxes have a role in conservation and wildlife-watching, but there is no guarantee a box will be used. Bats are rather sniffy about where they will sleep and take to boxes less enthusiastically than birds.

What makes the ideal bat box? Bat boxes take many shapes and sizes, but they must all be well-sealed and not draughty. The warmest area in the box is the top and this, in particular, needs to be draught-free and preferably insulated. There are numerous commercially available bat boxes available, but if you're making one yourself, the basic wooden wedge-shaped design suggested by the Bat Conservation Trust works better than most:

- All timber used in bat boxes should be rough-sawn to allow bats to cling and to climb. The wood must also be untreated, since bats are very sensitive to the chemicals used for timber treatment. A bat ladder – a backplate leading up into the box which is scored for easy gripping – is essential, as is an entry slit wide enough to admit bats but thin enough to keep out predators.
- The cutting plan is self-explanatory, except that the acute-angled ends of the triangular sides are cut off to give the entrance slot of the required width. The entrance should be about 20mm.
- The top edge of the back board and the rear edge of the roof must be bevelled to fit. The roof and back board are next to each other on the cutting plan so that, with a tilting circular

saw or jigsaw, the bevels can be cut in one go. The cutting angle is approximately 65 degrees.

- The front-opening door is pivoted at the bottom on two clout nails. A hole is drilled high up through one side of the box and into the side of the door. This takes a loose-fitting clout nail which holds the door firmly closed against the door stops. These are cut from a 10–12mm strip and are fitted at the top and sides of the door-opening to act as a door frame and aid weather-proofing.

- The side door stops are cut off about 3cm short of the bottom to allow freedom of movement of the door.

- A small screw is fitted as a knob for opening the door.

- The only other point is to ensure that the door is a loose fit to allow for the wood swelling – the door stops take care of the gaps. Gluing as well as nailing will ensure that there is the minimum of heat leakage. Extramite, an odourless wood glue, is recommended.

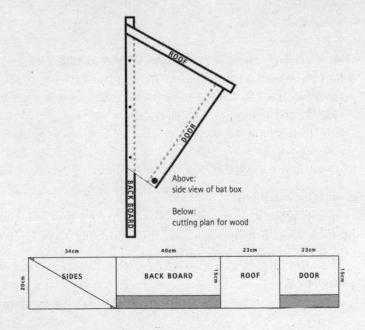

Above:
side view of bat box

Below:
cutting plan for wood

SITING CHECKLIST

Where is the most suitable location for your bat box? A bat box should be:

- Located in a place where bats are known to feed.
- Sheltered from strong winds.
- Exposed to sunlight for as much of the day as possible to increase the box's internal temperature.
- Positioned high up away from the reach of cats.
- Close to a hedge or tree line, as some species of bat use these to navigate and are reluctant to cross open spaces to get to and from roosts.
- Ideally, three boxes should be clustered together, facing in different directions, in order to allow bats to select a range of roosting temperatures at different times of year – preferably south, south-east and south-west. Try to avoid due west, as this is the prevailing direction of the wind and rain.

Tip: Identifying species of bats can be difficult, but bat detectors, which isolate bats' echolocation, are fun and useful for helping you to spot bats that you would otherwise miss. www.nhbs.com has a range of bat detectors and provides advice.

WILDLIFE TO WATCH OUT FOR

Brown long-eared bat
The species most likely to use bat boxes. They are easy to identify from their slow fluttering flight and their 'hovering' to pick insects off the leaves of garden trees and shrubs.

Pipistrelle bat
There are actually three types of pipistrelle in Britain: the common,

the soprano and the nathusius. All are brown, small and will fit in a medium matchbox. They like the space under the eaves of houses, so try not to block these off.

Daubenton's bat
A bat hawking over a garden pond is likely to be a daubenton's; they can actually seize insects coming off the water with their hobbit claws.

Noctule bat
Fairly easy to identify from its relatively large size, which is about that of a starling.

PROJECTS FOR SMALL SPACES: BUILD A WILDLIFE HOTEL

Made of recycled materials, a wildlife stack – a vertical hotel for mini-beasts – need cost nothing to make, will provide a lodging for hundreds of different species and, with just a touch of creativity, can look as though it's an attractive high-end design feature. It will also provide hours and hours of close-up wildlife watching. You can build as big (as long as it's safe) or as small as you want.

- Where possible, select a site that has dappled shade.
- The base needs to be firm. To build the stack place two bricks end to end on their sides and another two bricks parallel to these to create mini-'tramlines'.
- Place plywood or lengths of softwood across as a 'floor'.
- Repeat upwards, so you have a hotel with floors.
- To keep the stack dry, place roofing tiles or slates on the top floor, or cover the wood with roofing felt or polythene.
- Now fill the gaps between the floors with a variety of animal-friendly materials, one material per storey. Some suggested fillings are:
  - Straw.
  - Stones.

- Roofing tiles.
- Rolled-up sheets of corrugated cardboard (lacewings love these).
- Logs (best of all, logs with holes drilled in the ends).
- Pipes.
- Sand.
- Bamboo canes.
- Twigs.
- Hollow stems from hogweed (the ideal home for mason bees).

Quicker even than building with bricks and boards, if you have the space, is to create a wildlife stack with pallets. Pile on top of each other and tie.

BUMBLEBEE BOX

There are twenty-five species of bumblebee in the British Isles. The 'Big Six' species of bumblebee usually seen in gardens are the garden bumblebee, the common carder bee, the early bumblebee, the red-tailed, the buff-tailed and the white-tailed bumblebee. All the *Bombus* species have bulky bodies covered by hair.

Bumblebees are social insects and a nest in late summer will contain the old queen bee, who founded the colony, and young queens that will mate, over-winter and establish next year's colonies. Queen bees (which can be up to 30mm in length) are fertile females. The smaller worker bees are sterile females; workers gather nectar and pollen to feed the grubs, which are reared in wax cells in the nest.

In late summer the colony's new queen bees look for somewhere to hibernate, usually digging themselves a shallow underground chamber in which to winter. Try providing a hibernation den for queen bumblebees in your garden.

- Build a 100 x 100 x 200mm box with a lid, from untreated wood. Cut a small entrance hole, roughly 30mm wide, near the bottom of one side.
- During April, dig a hole in a dry, well-drained spot, preferably north-facing at the bottom of a hedge, rockery, fence or wall, and place the box inside.
- Push a rod or pipe (25–30mm wide) through the ground so that it meets up with the entrance hole in the box.
- Place bedding material such as dry grass or straw in the box, close the lid. Cover the box with logs, turf or a large stone.
- Plant a 10cm tall stick upright nearby as a 'marking post' to help bees find their way home.

Alternatively, use a 225mm deep clay flower pot. Bury this in a suitable location so that the drainage hole in the base is facing outwards. Attach a 5cm length of hosepipe to the drainage hole. Place bedding in the pot. Cover the pot with soil so that only the pipe is left sticking out.

A MASON BEE HOTEL

Unlike the highly social bumblebee, mason bees are solitary. After hatching in spring, the female looks for hollow stems in which to lay her eggs. If you can provide a hotel she'll quite possibly come to your garden. Welcome her with arms wide. Mason bees are extremely effective pollinators.

- Cut an untreated, approximately 10cm-wide plank into lengths to make a rectangular or triangular frame.
- Fix the frame together with screws.
- Cut stems of hogweed or other hollow-stemmed plants and fit into the frame, hollow-end out. Use rubber gloves to handle hogweed – the 'juice' can cause an allergic skin reaction.

- Pack the stems into the hotel until they 'lock' and don't shift around.
- Hang the hotel on a sunny, sheltered wall before March.

Hopefully the female mason bee will select one of the hollow stems and lay an egg inside, together with a store of pollen for the grub to eat when it hatches. This done, the bee seals the cell with a plug of mud, and starts the egg-laying process in another stem. The young bees won't emerge until the following year.

BIRD BOXES

Bird nestboxes in the garden have long been a source of human pleasure. They are also increasingly recognised as a helping hand that can make a difference as to whether a bird population thrives in a locality or is lost from it. Inner-city gardens, as well as suburban and country ones, can encourage a surprisingly diverse range of species. Kestrels and swifts are both noted users of artificial nest sites in city centres.

Remember that birds are cautious, and may well avoid your lovingly made nest box for years. This does not mean it is a wasted box. Birds roost in boxes as well as nest in them. As many as 50 wrens can squeeze into an unused small bird box in a cold snap.

STEP-BY-STEP: MAKE A BIRD BOX FOR SMALL AND MEDIUM-SIZED GARDEN BIRDS

Natural nests do not come in standard sizes, so use the plan below only as a guide. Any plank or sheet of 15mm thick untreated timber is suitable.

Step 1. Mark and saw the wood as per the plan. NB It gives measurements for both a small and a medium box, so use only the first

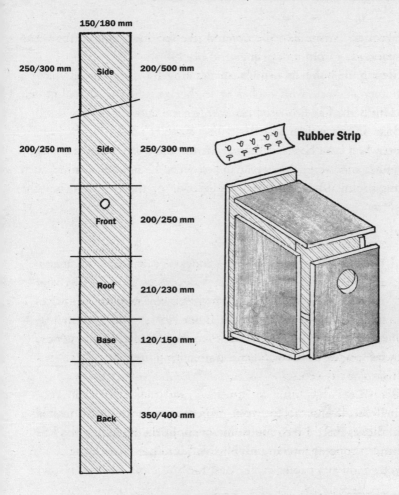

or the second figure. For starlings and thrushes, use the dimensions for the medium box; for tits and sparrows use the small one.

Step 2. Drill two or three drainage holes in the base of the box.

Step 3. Use galvanised screws to assemble.

Step 4. Drill the entrance hole. This needs to be at least 125mm from the base of the box. The size of the hole will depend on which species you wish to attract. As a rough guide: 25mm for blue and coal tits, 28mm for great tits and tree sparrows, 32mm for house sparrows, 45mm for starlings and blackbirds.

Step 5. Fix the lid with a metal hinge, or you could make a homemade one with rubber or leather attached with roofing felt clout nails. The box needs to open for autumn cleaning.

Step 6. Fasten with a catch.

Step 7. If your box is constructed from soft wood, paint the outside with a water-based preservative known to be safe for wildlife, such as Sadolin. Only apply to the exterior of the box, and not the entrance hole or inside.

Tip: Not all birds like a round entrance hole to their home. Robins, spotted flycatchers, pied wagtails and black redstarts, among other species, require an open front. So simply saw a third off the top of the front panel for these birds. The same birds can also be attracted by a nest box which is an integral part of a house wall, being a 'missing' brick with a low retaining edge.

If you do not believe your carpentry skills are up to making a bird box, there exist a multitude of suppliers, including the RSPB: http://shopping.rspb.org.uk/birds-wildlife/nestboxes.html. Or try your hand at a papier-mâché nest for house martins (see below).

SITING

To a large extent siting depends on the species the box is intended for. Boxes for tits should be fixed three to four metres up a tree or a wall. House sparrows and starlings will happily use nest boxes high up under the eaves. Open-fronted boxes for wrens and robins, on the other hand, need to be low down, below 2m, hidden among vegetation. Those for spotted flycatchers need to be about 2–4m high, also sheltered by vegetation.

Face the box, where possible, north and east away from strong sunlight and westerly winds. Make sure that the birds have a clear flight path to the nest. Tilt the box forwards slightly so that any driving rain won't enter through the hole.

Do not attach a perch – it will only give predators something to sit on.

It is always worth experimenting with the siting of boxes if they are unsuccessful; sometimes just an inch or two's change can mean occupation rather than avoidance.

Remember that some birds are colonial, and will more readily make a home in the garden if several boxes for their species are installed.

Don't forget to clean your nest boxes in autumn. Remove the old nests and clean the boxes with scalding hot water to kill parasites.

Tip: Provide suitable nest-building materials for birds. In spring, leave dog combings, straw and hay out in the garden. If you put out short lengths of natural-coloured wool, when you come to clean the nests in autumn you'll be able to see which birds used your materials.

STEP-BY-STEP: MAKE A PAPIER-MÂCHÉ NEST FOR HOUSE MARTINS

'This guest of summer,
The temple-haunting martlet, does approve,
By his loved masonry, that the heaven's breath
Smells wooingly here'
— *Macbeth*, William Shakespeare

House martins or 'martlets' are summer visitors to the UK, arriving in April and departing in October for wintering grounds in tropical

Africa. They nest colonially – in a flock – usually on buildings. House martins are easily distinguishable from swifts and swallows by their bright white rumps.

Nationally the house martin population appears to be undergoing a slow decline, with numbers down by as much as 40 per cent since the 1970s, probably due to lack of nest sites. To make their cup-shaped nests high under the eaves of buildings, house martins require mud. A bog garden will provide a ready supply of wet earth. Or you can give some house martins a pre-fab home by building a nest from papier-mâché.

Step 1. Buy a cheap children's plastic football 18cm in diameter. (A balloon works well too.)

Step 2. Mix 8 parts wallpaper paste to 1 part water.

Step 3. Dip strips of newspaper in the glue and 'plaster' onto the ball. Build up at least five layers, letting each layer dry before applying the next.

Step 4. When the papier-mâché is dry, cut the ball into quarters with a Stanley knife – just as though quartering a melon.

Step 5. Gently peel the plastic football quarters away from the papier-mâché.

Step 6. Make the entrance at the top of each quarter by cutting out a semi-circle, 6 x 2.5cm.

Step 7. For the back fixing, you need a piece of unplaned wood 30 x 20cm. Drill three holes, one in each of the top corners, and one in the bottom centre.

Step 8. Position the papier-mâché cup on the board, so the fixing holes are not obstructed. Now secure the cup to the board with at least five strips of papier-mâché inside and out. Leave to dry.

Step 9. If you are worried that the papier-mâché strips will not hold the cup in place, you can use strips of duct tape on the exterior.

Step 10. Paint with mud-coloured safe (water-based) paint.

Step 11. A smear of real mud on the outside wouldn't go amiss.

Step 12. Fix the board under the eaves of a north- or east-facing wall, so that the eaves form a lid. Fix several nest cups in a row for best results.

> **Tip:** Nest boxes for house martins should not be sited near those for house sparrows.

BIRD TABLE

The simple bird table is the heart of the wildlife garden. As well as a food station for feathered species, it is a focus of interest for the household, and the pleasure and interest it provides is almost boundless.

But the table needs to be positioned properly if birds are to use the table. Pick somewhere relatively open, away from overhanging branches where cats can lurk. Cats are the nemesis of garden birds.

STEP-BY-STEP: MAKE A BIRD TABLE

Use wood that will not disintegrate when wet – marine plywood from a sustainable source at least 12mm thick is ideal. Otherwise use softwood and treat with a safe water-based preservative such as Sadolin or Fenceguard. There is no minimum or maximum size for a bird table, but a small table will become overcrowded and argumentative, and shyer species will stay away. About 30 x 50cm is fine. A rim of 1cm beading will help prevent food being blown away.

Step 1. Cut a rectangle of 30 x 50 x 1.2cm wood.

Step 2. Cut 2 lengths of 29 x 1cm beading, and 2 lengths of 50 x 1cm beading.

Step 3. Glue and nail, with panel pins, the beading to the top of the rectangle, ensuring there is a 1cm gap at each end of the table.

Step 4. Several screw-in hooks in the edges of the table will be useful for hanging fat balls, or nut or seed feeders.

Step 5. Attach the board with brackets to an upright post of approx 1.5m in length.

Step 6. Fix the post into the ground. A sleeve dug into the earth consisting of a length of plastic pipe is useful if the table needs to be taken out for mowing. Alternatively, drill out a suitably sized hole in a large flat log and insert the post.

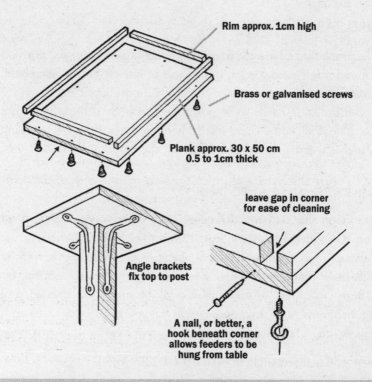

Rim approx. 1cm high

Brass or galvanised screws

Plank approx. 30 x 50 cm
0.5 to 1cm thick

Angle brackets
fix top to post

leave gap in corner
for ease of cleaning

A nail, or better, a
hook beneath corner
allows feeders to be
hung from table

Tip: Tie a large bunch of thorny foliage – holly or blackthorn is ideal – around the post to deter cats and squirrels from ascending to the feeding station.

OTHER FEEDERS FOR BIRDS

Seed feeders

Tubular transparent containers with holes, through which birds are able to access the seed, are inexpensive and widely available to buy. These feeders are designed for sunflower seeds and seed mixes labelled feeder seed. They will attract greenfinches, goldfinches, siskins and blue, great, and coal tits.

Nut feeders

Should be made of steel mesh since woodpecker tongues can get caught in plastic netting. A mesh gauge of 6mm is idea, small enough to retain the nuts, big enough to allow in a bird's bill.

Half-coconuts

A feeder that is fun for children to make (with adult supervision):

- Buy a coconut and a packet of suet.
- Hole the coconut at each end and let the milk drain out.
- Saw the coconut in half, sideways. Eat and drink contents!
- Thread thick string through the hole in each end, so the demi-coconut can be hung like a bell when ready.
- Put in 'bird pudding' to the two halves of the coconut. Allow to set.
- Hang from bird table or bracket on the wall.

Recipe for bird pudding

Take roughly equal parts of the following: dried fruits, chopped fresh fruit, nyjer seed, peanuts, cheese, oatmeal and brown breadcrumbs. Pour over melted suet and quickly mix. Pour into the halves of coconut, topping up with molten suet if necessary. Leave till the 'pudding' has solidified.

WHAT AND WHEN TO FEED BIRDS

About two thirds of British households feed the birds in winter. Most of us love doing this, but feeding can be expensive and the food provided not always suitable. With a little thought you can minimise the cost to your wallet – and the cost to the planet, because the ingredients in branded bird foods are sometimes imported from the furthest corners of the world.

So, ensure that feeding birds is part of the overall wildlife plan of the garden management of your garden. You should rely on wild foods as much as possible by 'growing your own' and planting berry-producing bushes and trees (see the bird border in chapter 4), and leaving the seed heads on 'weeds' and other flora. Fallen fruit should be left on the ground and not tidied away. Mulching flowerbeds with dead leaves in winter will keep worms and other invertebrates near the surface, providing valuable foraging for song thrushes and blackbirds.

Nevertheless, there will still be times when it is necessary to supplement the available wild diet of birds, and you can give yourself a pat on the back for doing so. There is an array of scientific evidence highlighting the positive effects of the provision of supplementary food for birds, not least in the over-winter survival rates of a number of species. And, of course, you may simply want to feed the birds for the enjoyment of it. In winter, key foods for birds are those high in fat and energy, such as sunflower hearts, black sunflower seeds, nyjer or thistle seed, peanuts and fat balls, all of which can be readily purchased. Mild cheese and porridge oats are a good standby, as are sultanas (soaked first in water) and over-ripe tree fruits (likely to be found in many a kitchen fridge or cupboard) for ground feeding blackbirds. Live mealworms (actually the larval stage of beetles) will be seized on by wrens, robins and blackbirds. Live mealworms can be bought from many bird food suppliers.

Tip: Proprietary seed mixes vary vastly in content and quality. Cheap mixes often have a high proportion of cereal, which is favoured by pigeons and sparrows. The best mixes are carefully balanced to cater for a range of species. Both the RSPB and the British Trust for Ornithology (BTO) sell a variety of seed mixes through shops and online. Goldfinches have a predilection for nyjer seed, while almost all finches and tits can be tempted by sunflower hearts.

Try to balance the amount of food that you provide with the number of birds coming into the garden to feed. In this way you will avoid creating a food surplus – which will either go off and perhaps become a health hazard for birds, or attract rats. Good practice is to remove droppings and any unwanted food from the bird table each night.

Conservationists increasingly recommend supplementary feeding for birds over the course of the year, not just in winter. Certainly, if the breeding season is especially cold or wet you should consider filling the feeders and putting food on the table. But NEVER feed birds white bread or desiccated coconut (which both swell up inside the bird's stomach), or salty household scraps (which can cause severe dehydration in small birds).

Tip: To feed song and mistle thrushes, blackbirds, redwings and fieldfares, buy old fruit from markets and spread around and over the lawn.

Feeding birds: A checklist

- Maximise the benefit to birds by growing thorny climbers by the pole supporting the table, which will prevent cats, rats and squirrels from leaping onto the table. Losing food to rats and squirrels is feeding the enemy.

- Ensure you are not making it easier for birds of prey to catch your birds. It's wonderful to see a kestrel or sparrowhawk swoop and take a bird – but you don't want to only be feeding falcons and hawks. Place feeders away from trees and fences which might hide the approach of birds of prey.
- Try to buy high-quality food from reputable suppliers.
- Good hygiene is imperative to prevent disease and illness, so remove droppings and any unwanted food from the bird table each night and sterilise feeders regularly. (The fluids used for sterilising baby feeding equipment are ideal.)
- Don't put out too much seed at a time. Old seed can go mouldy, increasing the risks of disease, so aim to top up your feeders regularly.
- Birds also need to drink, so keep a bird bath or another shallow container topped up. An upturned dustbin lid is ideal.

Tip: If you have a tree or trees in the garden, tuck small parcels of fatty food in the cracks and holes in the bark for treecreepers, nuthatches, wrens and tits.

A HEDGEHOG HOME

Hedgehogs need somewhere to hibernate in winter, so why not provide them with a snug home? They are undemanding creatures, and they will readily go to sleep in a pile of leaves in the bottom of a beech hedge, in a log pile, or in a compost heap. A purpose-built 'hedgehog house' has much to recommend it, however, being secure against predators.

Much the easiest way to make a hedgehog house is to persuade your local vintner to give you a wine crate. Otherwise, you need to construct a wooden box 40 x 30 x 40cm from sustainable, untreated wood. Then:

- With a jigsaw cut an entrance hole 11 x 15cm on one side at the base.
- Drill a hole in the opposite side near the top for a 30cm length of hose to fit through. Insert the hose.
- Position the box somewhere sheltered and quiet in the garden. The bottom of a hedge, a shady corner, the base of a rockery or behind the greenhouse are good places. The entrance should face south. A house with a cold north wind blowing through the front door is unlikely to be occupied.
- Cover with logs, branches, soil and leaves, but leave the entrance clear.
- Now make an approach tunnel to the entrance, with two parallel lines of bricks, set so a hedgehog can squeeze through – they need about 10cm square. Six bricks should be sufficient. Cover the roof with slates or roof tiles, and weigh these down with stones.
- The tunnel entrance is to stop predators, especially foxes, from breaking in.
- Do not be tempted to line the house with bedding. This is a job the Tiggy-Winkles like to do themselves. It is part of the hibernation ritual.

WATCHING WILDLIFE

The windows of the house or garden shed make a good observation point for watching garden wildlife. Animals have difficulty in seeing through glass. If you're outdoors, sit very still. What alarms animals is movement.

There is great fun in making a hide, which in children's language is a den. More than one large cardboard box of the sort containing white goods has been remade as a bird hide. A peep-hole cut in the side, a camouflage paint-job with green-and-brown poster paint, and the job is done. Leave it for a day or two in situ for the birds and animals to get used to it before a child sits inside as a tyro David Attenborough.

A green tarpaulin over a basic wooden pole frame works wonders, as does an old tent, while proper 'camo netting' as used by the army is widely available to buy.

Night is a good time to view amphibians. Shine a powerful torch on the pond or a less powerful one under logs and large stones. Large mammals can be observed by putting a red filter over an outdoor light. Most mammals are not disturbed by red light. To know what small mammals are in the garden you may need to use a 'footprint tube'.

Tip: Always keep the binoculars handy. Birds and animals can vanish with frustrating speed.

DO-IN-AN-HOUR: MAKE A SMALL MAMMAL FOOTPRINT TUBE

Many small garden mammals, such as wood mice, are nocturnal or lurk in the undergrowth and are frustratingly difficult to observe. One gloriously easy way of finding out which small mammals are living in or visiting the garden is to make a footprint tube, a harmless device which takes impressions of animal tracks.

To make a footprint tube:

- Cut a 45mm plastic overflow pipe (available from any DIY shop) into a 30cm length.
- Then cut a piece of paper to fit along the bottom length of the tube as though it was 'gutter'.
- Staple a 7 x 4cm rectangle of greaseproof paper widthways to both ends of the paper – these rectangles will be 'inkpads'.
- Mix equal amounts of non-toxic children's poster paint with vegetable oil and daub thickly onto the greaseproof paper.

Plastic piping
30cm long, 4.5cm diameter

Inkpad – tracking substance
painted on greaseproof paper

© The Mammal Society

Sheet of plain paper

- Place a piece of chocolate or lump of peanut butter in the centre of the paper gutter and slide into the tube.
- Put in the garden under a bush and leave overnight.
- Next day, slide out the paper and see what tracks have been left behind.

RECORDING WILDLIFE

Keep a nature diary of observations and first sightings. This will help you understand the wildlife in your garden, so you can manage it even better.

A wall calendar of key events in the garden wildlife cycle is a good starting place. When did the house martins arrive? The frogs spawn? The hawthorn blossom?

You may also want to take part in local or national recording schemes. Sometimes known as 'citizen science projects', these surveys contribute enormously to the overall understanding of our environment such as the RSPB's 'State of Nature report'. They are also jolly good fun. All you need is a little time, a notebook and enthusiasm.

MONITORING SCHEMES

Birds

The UK is home to the world's largest wildlife survey: the RSPB's Big Garden Birdwatch, held annually over a weekend in January. The public are asked to record which birds visit their garden during an hour and the results help the charity understand the health of our garden birds. The Big Garden Birdwatch in 2013 received an enormous 590,000 records. See www.rspb.org.uk/birdwatch.

The British Trust for Ornithology's Garden BirdWatch records birds in the garden (and other wildlife) weekly over the course of a year. See www.bto.org/volunteer-surveys/gbw/about.

Butterflies and moths

Launched in 2010, the Big Butterfly Count requires you to count butterflies for just 15 minutes in summer. Run by Butterfly Conservation, who helpfully provide a downloadable identification chart at www.bigbutterflycount.org.

The same charity also runs National Moth Night. You can view moths any way you choose, by using a moth-trap, going out with a torch or by sitting at the kitchen window with the light on. For more information visit www.mothnightinfo.

Mammals

The People's Trust for Endangered Species runs an annual Living with Mammals survey, with recording done between 1 April and 30 June each year. See www.ptes.org.

For those with more time, there are also ongoing monitoring schemes of vulnerable species.

One of the simplest ways to help scientists understand the fate of the UK's fauna and flora is to conduct a twenty-four hour survey called a BioBlitz. You can do a BioBlitz at any time, or if you want to join the crowd a mass garden BioBlitz takes place over the first weekend in June. See www.bioblitzuk.org.uk.

CHAPTER 10
THE WILDLIFE GARDEN YEAR

SPRING – MARCH TO MAY

The garden 'springing' to life after winter always seems like a minor miracle. The days are lengthening, the birds are singing and hedges are greening. Trees are in blossom and woodland wildflowers in bloom.

Blackbirds and robins are among the earliest nesters, in the hope they can squeeze two or three broods into the year. Early nesters, though, can suffer from sparseness of cover to conceal nests and a scarcity of food. Include some evergreens among your plants, and keep feeding the birds.

TASKS

- Pile up dry plant stems you left standing in autumn, so the insects can emerge.
- Sow a wildflower meadow.
- Sow seeds of hardy annuals.
- Plant your summer-flowering bulbs.
- Plant shrubs and perennials.
- Feed and mulch beds and borders.
- Plant summer bulbs.
- Plant container-grown shrubs.
- Plant hanging baskets and containers.
- Sow vegetable crops outdoors including salad crops, cabbages and peas.

- Feed emerging hedgehogs with specialist food (obtainable from many nurseries or online); at a pinch, they can be fed cat food.
- Hang out bits of wool for birds to make nests with; if you use coloured yarns you'll be able to track which birds used your offerings.
- Put out bee boxes.
- Mow lawn until March/April.
- When frosts have passed, plant out tomatoes and courgettes.

WILDLIFE TO WATCH OUT FOR

Male birds will be in full song. Listen out in particular for the blackcap – the warbler poet John Clare termed the 'March nightingale' (although its call is altogether less melodious than a nightingale and sounds like two pebbles being clicked together).

Toads will be mating.

Hedgehogs, bats and butterflies, will emerge from hibernation.

Orange-tip butterflies will be on the wing from April.

The nesting season for birds is in full swing, reaching its peak for most garden birds in May.

Summer birds will be arriving from April onwards.

SUMMER – JUNE TO AUGUST

TASKS

- Spread a mulch of compost or shredded bark around trees, shrubs and roses when the soil is moist.
- Sow vegetable crops directly into the soil, and try some in large pots.
- Go pond dipping with children.
- Water the compost heap during dry weather.
- Keep the pond and bird baths topped up with stored rainwater.
- Clear the pond of green algae or blanket weed.

- In June, cut spring-flowering meadows and cut for rest of summer.
- Cut summer-flowering meadows at end of July or in August.
- Dead-head flowers to keep them flowering longer.
- Hoe unwanted weeds.
- Put out 'hotels' for beneficial insects.
- Relax and enjoy the garden and its wildlife.

WILDLIFE TO WATCH OUT FOR

Adult great spotted woodpeckers escorting juveniles into the garden to show them food sources.

All birds will be energetically feeding their young.

High summer is the peak season for butterflies and moths on the wing.

'Cuckoo-spit' will be in long grass.

Tadpoles will be metamorphosing into frogs in the pond.

AUTUMN – SEPTEMBER TO OCTOBER

TASKS

- Dead-head summer flowers to keep them flowering longer.
- Leave seed heads to over-winter to provide food for birds.
- Leave dry plant stems standing (until spring). All manner of insects will crawl inside to winter.
- Give late-flowering meadows a cut, but not below 5cm.
- Animals start preparing for hibernation, so leave out food for hedgehogs.
- If you are having a bonfire, check carefully for hedgehogs first.
- Provide a home for a hedgehog to hibernate – a leaf mould pile, compost heap, log pile, an accessible space under a shed or a hedgehog home are all favourite places.
- Drill holes in wood to make hibernation holes for leafcutter bees.
- In October, begin winter pruning.

- Spread dead leaves over flower border to provide foraging habitat for the thrush family.
- Surplus dead leaves can be piled up in a sheltered position or put in temporary bins made from chicken wire. Alternatively, put leaves in black bin sacks (with holes) and allow to rot down.
- But try not to rake all the autumn leaves from your lawn as they will soon be drawn underground by earthworms. Earthworms help aerate lawns and decompose organic material. They are also an important part of the diet of numerous birds, including the blackbird and song thrush.
- Clean the bird table and feeders with a sterilising solution (anything used for babies is fine), and remove old nests from nest boxes. Scald the inside of the boxes with boiling water to kill parasites.
- Now is a good time to dig out a pond.
- It's also the time to dredge existing ponds. Hack and pull out excessive growth of pond plants.
- Put a net over the pond to prevent leaves falling in.
- Dig new beds before frosts arrive. Robins and other birds will pick over the upturned earth for invertebrates.
- Plant spring bulbs between September and November.
- Plant out spring-flowering bedding plants.
- Plant out potted wildflowers on the lawn.
- Plant bare-root and balled shrubs, trees and hedges from November (until March).
- Plant soft fruit bushes – they will be ready to establish by next season.

WILDLIFE TO WATCH OUT FOR

The last of the summer migrant birds will be flying south, while redwings, fieldfares and other thrushes will be arriving. Waxwings may also visit the garden to strip bushes and hedges of berries.

Hedgehogs, newts, snakes, lizards, bats and many insects will be starting hibernation.

Spiders' webs, drenched in dew, are to be seen in the grass and hedges; the webs in the grass are mostly made by money spiders; a large unmown lawn might contain several thousand of them.

WINTER – NOVEMBER TO FEBRUARY

The worse the winter and the less the food in the countryside, the more important the garden becomes.

TASKS

- Feed birds food with high fat content – it helps keep them warm. Feed regularly so birds do not waste vital time and energy making fruitless (or nutless, or seedless) visits to a table.
- Put fat blocks in wire cages – not plastic netting as sometimes birds get feet caught in them (or tongues in the case of woodpeckers).
- Remember birds are most vulnerable at the end of winter when they have to begin singing and staking out their territories.
- Make sure water for birds is not frozen.
- Plant berry and fruiting trees such as *Pyracantha*, crab apple (*Malus*), rowan (*Sorbus aucuparia)* and *Cotoneaster*.
- Buy a Christmas tree with roots, and plant in the garden after your celebrations. Coal tits and goldcrests can use it for roosting.
- Crumble left-over Christmas cake and put out for the birds. But it may be sensible to hold back on any Christmas cake absolutely chokka with brandy, sherry or other types of hooch. A tablespoonful or so in a cake will not affect the birds.
- Plan and dig new borders and beds.
- Plant a native mixed hedge.

- Prune apple and fruit trees which are now dormant.
- Trim hedges once the berries have been eaten; preferably trim one side of the hedge and leave the other side until next year.
- Dig the vegetable plot, incorporate the contents of the compost heap.
- Take hardwood cuttings.
- Mend and replace fences and arches.
- Check and repair nest boxes. Put new nest boxes up, so that birds will get used to them before the nesting season. They also make good winter roosts.
- Make New Year's Resolutions to increase your wildlife gardening.
- Join in the RSPB's Big Garden Birdwatch.

WILDLIFE TO WATCH OUT FOR

Male robins will be driving intruders from their patch. Unusual visitors are likely to be seen on the bird table, such as greater spotted woodpeckers, fieldfares, redwings, bramblings and redpolls.

Frogs spawn from February onwards.

Some early bumblebees will be taking wing.

RESOURCES

USEFUL ORGANISATIONS

Bat Conservation Trust www.bats.org.uk
British Trust for Ornithology www.bto.org
Butterfly Conservation www.butterfly-conservation.org
Dry Stone Walling Association www.dswa.org.uk
Flora Locale www.floralocale.org
London Wildlife Trust www.wildlondon.org.uk
Natural England www.naturalengland.org.uk
Pond Conservation www.pondconservation.org.uk
Plantlife International www.plantlife.org.uk
Royal Horticultural Society www.rhs.org.uk
Royal Society for the Protection of Birds www.rspb.org.uk
The Conservation Volunteers www.tcv.org.uk
The Wildlife Trusts www.wildlifetrusts.org

SUPPLIERS

Food, Nesting Boxes, Naturalist Equipment
BTO /Ernest Charles 0800 7316 770
  www.birdfoodsdirect.com
NHBS 01803 865913 www.nhbs.com
RSPB 0845 1 200 501 or 01324 744 341
  http://shopping.rspb.org.uk
The Specialist Bird Food Company 01420 23986
  www.wild-bird-food.co.uk

Plants and Seeds
British Wildflower Plants 01603 716615 www.wildflowers.co.uk
Really Wild Flowers 01444 413376 www.reallywildflowers.co.uk
For readymade sedum matting or tiles:
  Enviromat 0333 456 4526 www.enviromat.co.uk
  Sedum Green Roof 01747 830176 www.sedumgreenroof.co.uk

INDEX